State Support of
International Terrorism

State Support of International Terrorism

Legal, Political, and Economic Dimensions

John F. Murphy

Westview Press
BOULDER • SAN FRANCISCO

Mansell Publishing Limited
LONDON

Excerpt on pp. 92–93 copyright © 1976 by The New York Times Company. Reprinted by permission.

Published in 1989 in the United States of America by Westview Press, Inc., 5500 Central Avenue, Boulder, Colorado 80301

Published in 1989 in Great Britain by Mansell Publishing Ltd., *A Cassell Imprint,* Artillery House, Artillery Row, London SW1P 1RT, England

Library of Congress Cataloging-in-Publication Data
Murphy, John Francis, 1937–
  State support of international terrorism : legal, political, and economic dimensions / John F. Murphy.
    p. cm.
  Includes bibliographical references.
  ISBN 0-8133-0861-5
  1. Terrorism—Government policy. I. Title.
HV6431.M87   1989
363.3′2—dc20   89-36171
                                                                                  CIP

British Library Cataloguing in Publication Data
Murphy, John F. (John Francis), 1937–
  State support of international terrorism: legal, political, and economic dimensions
1. International terrorism. Organisation. Role of governments.
I. Title
322.4′2
ISBN 0-7201-2015-2

Printed and bound in the United States of America

The paper used in this publication meets the requirements of the American National Standard for Permanence of Paper for Printed Library Materials Z39.48-1984.

10   9   8   7   6   5   4   3   2   1

Contents

Acknowledgments

A number of people have been very helpful to me in writing this monograph. I want to acknowledge their assistance, on the understanding that the views expressed in this study are solely my own.

First and foremost, I want to express my appreciation to Richard E. Friedman, chair of the American Bar Association's Standing Committee on Law and National Security, for his support and his patience in allowing me an extension of time in which to complete this study. I am also grateful to the standing committee for its permission to publish this study.

Keith Highet, member of the New York bar and former president of the American Society of International Law, very kindly appointed me chair of the society's Committee on Responses to State-Sponsored Terrorism. The deliberations of the committee on many of the subjects covered in this book were exceedingly helpful in clarifying my own thinking and in giving me valuable information and insights.

Richard Hayes and Dewey Covington of Defense Systems, Inc., McClean, Virginia, generously shared with me some of their creative thinking on a possible typology of state support and state sponsorship of terrorism.

The secretarial staff of the Villanova University School of Law worked with good humor on many drafts of the chapters of this study. I am especially grateful for the highly competent and cheerful work of Terri LaVerghetta. Work on this study was also materially assisted by a research grant from the Villanova University School of Law in the summer of 1987.

John F. Murphy
Villanova, Pennsylvania

Introduction

Few would dispute that a major factor contributing to the world community's difficulties in combatting international terrorism is the lack of cooperation among states. This failure to act in concert is tantamount to state support of international terrorism because it fosters a milieu in which terrorism flourishes.

This is not the kind of state support of international terrorism, however, that has captured the headlines, which instead focus on the terrorism that has become a kind of surrogate warfare, used as a substitute for more conventional means. States unfriendly to the United States and other Western democracies especially follow this path: Iran, some have claimed,[1] is the archetypal case. Allegedly, Iran has trained, equipped, and harbored terrorists and has directed armed attacks, some of which could be defined as terrorist, against U.S. nationals. Similar claims have recently been made with respect to Libya, Syria, and other states.

Taking a broader view, some have alleged that the U.S. government itself is a major sponsor of international terrorism. Those observers cite as examples the U.S. training and financing of the Contras and the Central Intelligence Agency's role in preparing training manuals endorsing the assassination of Nicaraguan civilians, the provision of arms to Iran in exchange for hostages, and the unconditional provision of military assistance to Israel despite its "terrorist" policies against Palestinians in the occupied territories.[2]

It will not be the purpose of this book to explore the evidence to evaluate the correctness of these charges. As we shall see later, one of the difficulties in combatting state supported terrorism is that the process for gathering pertinent information is grossly unsatisfactory. Moreover—and more important—it is my firm belief that the rhetoric on this subject should be softened, lest it generate more heat than light and undermine rather than support efforts to combat state support of terrorism. To this end, I have made every effort to develop a typology of state support and state sponsorship of terrorism that minimizes reference to specific states. Rather the focus will be on individuals' particular acts that might be perceived as international terrorism and on states' acts that might be perceived as state support. The thesis of this book is that state support of terrorism is illegal and immoral, whatever state engages in such actions.

The effort, in other words, is to approach the subject of state support of international terrorism in as impartial a manner as possible. My goal is to suggest definitions of "international terrorism," "state support," and "state sponsorship" that in no way depend on political ideology.

Nevertheless, analysis in the abstract has its limitations, and concrete examples render discussion more meaningful. I have therefore referred on occasion to specific states in the section dealing with countermeasures against state sponsors of terrorism because some states have been targeted for such action in the past. For example, in Chapter 5, which addresses economic sanctions, I refer to Iran, Libya, and Syria, each of which has been subjected to economic sanctions for alleged sponsorship of terrorism.

Chapters 1 and 2 deal with the daunting problems of defining international terrorism and state support of international terrorism. In Chapter 3 I consider what steps might be taken to improve the gathering of information regarding international terrorism and state support of it. In Chapters 4 through 6 I review possible responses to state support of international terrorism, discussed in ascending order of coerciveness. They include quiet diplomacy; public protest; international and transnational claims; economic sanctions; and military responses. The primary focus is on the legal aspects of these responses, but political, economic, and cultural dimensions are also discussed insofar as they bear on the feasibility of the possible response. A concluding chapter sets forth my conclusions and recommendations.

Notes

1. *See, e.g.,* Bernstein, *In the U.S. War on Terrorism, Iran Is the Enemy,* The Heritage Foundation, Backgrounder (Sept. 3, 1985).

2. *See generally,* R. Falk, Revolutionaries and Functionaries (1988).

1

"International Terrorism": The Definitional Quagmire

Walter Laqueur, a leading commentator on terrorism, recently pointed out that 109 different definitions of the term were advanced between 1936 and 1981, and more have appeared since, including a half dozen provided by the U.S. government.[1] None of these definitions has been adopted by the world community. Efforts in the academic world to reach agreement on a definition have been equally unavailing.

In practice, the terms "terrorism" and "terrorists" have been used by politicians as labels to pin on their enemies. The cliché "One man's terrorist is another man's freedom fighter" is a notorious reflection of this game of semantics. This practice and other reasons once led the late Richard Baxter, professor of law at Harvard University and judge on the International Court of Justice, to remark, "We have cause to regret that a legal concept of 'terrorism' was ever inflicted upon us. The term is imprecise; it is ambiguous; and above all, it serves no operative legal purpose."[2] The substance of Judge Baxter's remarks is compelling, and from an ideal perspective, a strong argument could be made that the world community should stop using the term "terrorism" entirely. However, we must live in the real rather than an ideal world, and it is too late in the day for the ideal approach. Accordingly, we will consider some of the primary proposals for definition that have been advanced, evaluate their usefulness, and attempt to develop a working definition for purposes of this book.

This chapter provides first a brief historical background of the alternative approaches to definition and then considers definitions advanced by governments. These governmental definitions are found at the global, regional, and bilateral levels (in treaties or resolutions of international organizations) and at the national level (in legislation or in policy statements). Examined next are definitions advanced in the private sector by individual scholars or groups such as the International Law Association. The chapter concludes with my thoughts on the appropriate definitional approach for this book.

Historical Background

The word "terror" was first used in connection with the Jacobin "Reign of Terror" following the French Revolution.[3] Some governments even today would confine the definition to government action only, so-called state terrorism. As we shall see, however, this approach has relatively few supporters. Today the term "terrorism" is primarily applied to actions by private individuals or groups.

Until relatively recently, actions by individuals that today would be described as "terrorist" were subsumed under different labels. For example, assassinations, especially of a head of state, have a long history; only recently have they been treated as terrorist acts. As Professor Robert Friedlander has pointed out, the word "assassin" derives from Arabic and literally translated means "hashish-eater" or "one addicted to hashish."[4] Acting under the influence of drugs, Moslem assassins murdered prominent Christians and other religious enemies at the end of the Middle Ages.

Assassination was a prime weapon of the anarchist movement that reached its height at the end of the nineteenth century. Revolting against the state and other manifestations of authority, anarchists had succeeded in assassinating ten national leaders by the turn of the century.[5] Closely aligned with anarchism was the doctrine of revolutionary syndicalism. As influenced by the writings of Georges Sorel, this doctrine stressed the reformation of society through a militant working class and the general strike, as well as the moral purification of revolutionary violence.[6]

As applied to actions by individuals, the term "terrorism" was apparently used for the first time in an international penal instrument at the Third (Brussels) International Conference for the Unification of Penal Law held on June 26–30, 1930, in response to an increase in terrorist activity following World War I.[7] This interest in terrorism intensified with the assassination at Marseilles on October 9, 1934, of King Alexander of Yugoslavia and Louis Barthou, foreign minister of the French Republic, and led to the League of Nations drafting the Convention for the Prevention and Punishment of Terrorism.[8] This convention defined terrorism broadly to include "criminal acts directed against a state and intended to or calculated to create a state of terror in the minds of particular persons, or a group of persons, or the general public."[9] The convention received only one ratification and one accession and never came into force. In large part this may have been because of the approach of World War II, but it has also been suggested that a number of states were reluctant to ratify the convention because of the breadth of its definition of terrorism.[10] In any event, since it was not listed among the treaties and conventions for which the League was a depository and with respect to which the United Nations had taken any responsibility, the convention sank into obscurity.

Besides declining to revive the League convention, the United Nations made no attempt to replace it with one of its own. However, a similarly broad approach to the problem was taken by the International Law Commission in its 1954 Draft Code of Offenses Against the Peace and Security of Mankind.[11] The draft code, moreover, introduced the concept of state sponsorship—"the undertaking or encouragement by the authorities of a State, or the toleration by the authorities of a State of organized activities calculated to carry out terrorist acts in another State" was declared to be an offense against the peace and security of mankind and a crime under international law.[12] The General Assembly deferred consideration of the draft code pending agreement on a general definition of aggression, finally reached in 1974. Work on the draft code resumed, but has not yet produced a final agreement despite thirty-five years that have passed since 1954.

The kidnapping and killing at Munich on September 6, 1972, of eleven Israeli Olympic competitors by Arab terrorists, as well as a number of other spectacular acts of terrorism, resulted in a more narrowly focused approach: The United States on September 25 introduced a Draft Convention for the Prevention and Punishment of Certain Acts of International Terrorism.[13] In proposing the convention and in subsequent debates, U.S. representatives attempted to alleviate the concern of some member states that the convention was directed against wars of national liberation, pointing out that its coverage was limited to "any person who unlawfully kills, causes serious bodily harm or kidnaps another person." They noted further that these acts had to meet four separate conditions before the terms of the convention applied: First, the act had to be committed or take effect outside the territory of a state of which an alleged offender was a national. Second, the act had to be committed or take effect outside the state against which the act was directed, unless such acts were knowingly directed against a nonnational of that state. (Under this provision, an armed attack in the passenger lounge of an international airport would be covered.) Third, the act must not be committed either by or against a member of the armed forces of a state in the course of military hostilities. And fourth, the act had to be intended to damage the interests of or obtain concessions from a state or an international organization. Accordingly, U.S. representatives pointed out, certain controversial activities arguably terrorist in nature—such as fedayeen attacks in Israel against Israeli citizens and a wide range of activities by armed forces in Indochina and in southern Africa—were deliberately excluded from the convention's coverage. A particularly broad loophole was the first requirement about the identity of the alleged offender's state, a provision that excluded from the convention's scope most terrorist attacks in Latin America and elsewhere against transnational business personnel and facilities. As to persons allegedly committing offenses covered by the convention and apprehended in their territories, the draft required states adopting the convention to establish severe penalties for covered acts and either to prosecute such persons or extradite them to another state party for prosecution. Whether to prosecute or extradite the alleged offender was a decision left to the sole discretion of the apprehending state.

The U.S. draft resolution accompanying the draft convention requested that the General Assembly convene a plenipotentiary conference in early 1973 for the purpose of adopting the convention, call upon all states as a matter of urgency to become parties to and implement the International Civil Aviation Organization (ICAO) conventions on hijacking of and other offenses against aircraft (discussed in the next section), and request ICAO to draft as an urgent matter a convention on arrangements to enforce the principles of the conventions.[14] From the outset, however, it was apparent that the U.S. initiative faced substantial opposition from the Arab states, China, and a block of African states. In the general debate this opposition was expressed in perhaps its most extreme form by the Libyan representative, who described the United States initiative as a "ploy . . . against the legitimate struggle of the people under the yoke of colonialism and alien domination" and warned against the United Nations becoming "an instrument in local elections campaigns and a pawn of international propaganda based on falsehood and deceit."[15]

Despite several efforts to reach a compromise, the U.S. initiative failed. On December 11, 1972, the Sixth Committee (Legal) of the General Assembly adopted a draft resolution submitted by Algeria and other cosponsors by a vote of 76 to 34 (including the United States), with 16 abstentions. On December 18 the assembly approved the committee's decision by adopting Resolution 3034(XXVII) by a vote of 76 to 35 (U.S.), with 17 abstentions. Though the resolution expressed "*deep concern* over increasing acts of violence which endanger or take innocent human lives or jeopardize fundamental freedoms" and invited states to become parties to existing conventions on international terrorism and to take appropriate measures at the national level to eliminate it, the resolution's primary focus was on "finding just and peaceful solutions to the underlying causes which give rise to such acts of violence." The resolution also "[*r*]*eaffirms* the inalienable right to self-determination and independence of all peoples under the colonial and racist regimes and other forms of alien domination and upholds the legitimacy of their struggle." By way of implementation the resolution invited states to study the problem on an urgent basis and submit their observations to the secretary-general by April 10, 1973, and established an ad hoc committee, to be appointed by the president of the General Assembly, to study these observations and to submit a report with recommendations for elimination of the problem to the 28th session of the General Assembly.[16] The committee was appointed, but after meeting from July 16 through August 10, 1973, it reported that it was unable to agree on any recommendations for dealing with the problem.

Modern Developments

Global

The U.S. draft convention was the last attempt to define international terrorism in a binding international legal instrument. In place of these efforts the United Nations or its specialized agencies have adopted treaty provisions aimed at suppressing aircraft hijacking;[17] unlawful acts against the safety of civil aviation[18] or of airports serving international civil aviation;[19] unlawful acts against internationally protected persons, including diplomatic agents;[20] taking of hostages;[21] theft of nuclear material;[22] and unlawful acts against the safety of maritime navigation.[23] Although these treaty provisions are often loosely described as "antiterrorist," the acts they cover are criminalized regardless of whether, in a particular case, they could be described as "terrorism." All of these conventions require that a state party apprehending an alleged offender in its territory either extradite the person or submit the case to its own authorities for purposes of prosecution.

On December 9, 1985, the General Assembly adopted a resolution[24] that Vernon A. Walters, U.S. ambassador to the United Nations, described as "a symbol of new times."[25] Adopted by consensus, the resolution loosely defines terrorism as acts "which endanger or take innocent human lives, jeopardize fundamental freedoms, and seriously impair the dignity of human beings." In its operative paragraphs, it "[u]nequivocally *condemns*, as criminal, all acts, methods and practices of terrorism wherever and by whomever committed, including those which jeopardize friendly relations among States and their security"; invites states "[t]o take all appropriate measures at the national level . . . such as the harmonization of domestic legislation with existing international conventions, the fulfillment of assumed international obligations, and the prevention of the preparation and organization in their respective territories of acts directed against other States"; calls upon states "to fulfill their obligations under international law to refrain from organizing, instigating, assisting or participating in terrorist acts in other States, or acquiescing in activities within their territory directed towards the commission of such acts"; appeals to all states to become parties to the existing antiterrorist conventions; and urges all states:

to cooperate with one another more closely, especially through the exchange of relevant information concerning the prevention and combatting of terrorism, apprehension and prosecution or extradition of the perpetrators of such acts, the conclusion of special treaties and/or the incorporation into appropriate bilateral treaties of special clauses, in particular regarding the extradition or prosecution of terrorists.

Some have claimed that the provision in the resolution reaffirming "the inalienable right to self-determination" should be interpreted to permit "national liberation groups" to engage in terrorism as part of their struggle against "colonial and racist regimes and other forms of alien domination." However, the same provision provides that the struggle of national liberation movements must be conducted "in accordance with the purposes and principles of the Charter and of the Declaration on Principles of International Law Concerning Friendly Relations and Co-operation Among States in accordance with the Charter of the United Nations." The UN Charter implicitly and the Declaration on Principles of International Law Concerning Friendly Relations and Co-operation Among States[26] explicitly prohibit recourse to terrorism.

Most recently the UN General Assembly adopted a Declaration on the Enhancement of the Effectiveness of the Principle of Refraining from the Threat or Use of Force in International Relations.[27] Although the declaration does not contain a definition of terrorism, it does call upon states to cooperate at the bilateral, regional, and international levels in order to prevent and combat international terrorism and to "contribute actively to the elimination of causes underlying international terrorism." It further provides that states should fulfill their obligations under international law to refrain from organizing, instigating, assisting, or participating in paramilitary, terrorist, or subversive acts in other states, or acquiescing in organized activities within their territory directed toward the commission of such acts.

Regional

Three regional conventions have been adopted in an effort to combat international terrorism. These include the Convention to Prevent and Punish the Acts of Terrorism Taking the Form of

Crimes Against Persons and Related Extortion That Are of International Significance (OAS Convention),[28] the European Convention on the Suppression of Terrorism (European Convention),[29] and the Agreement on the Application of the European Convention for the Suppression of Terrorism (Dublin Agreement).[30] None of these conventions attempts to define international terrorism. Rather, like the conventions concluded under the auspices of the United Nations and its specialized agencies, these regional conventions focus on particular actions and the protection of particular targets from attack.

For example, Article 1 of the OAS Convention obligates states that are parties to cooperate "to prevent and punish acts of terrorism, especially kidnapping, murder and other assaults against the life or physical integrity of those persons to whom the state has the duty according to international law to give special protection, as well as extortion in connection with those crimes." Although there is a question as to the precise scope of this convention, its basic focus is on the protection of diplomats.

Nor does the European Convention, an antiterrorist initiative, attempt to define international terrorism. Its approach is to list a series of crimes that states that are parties are to exclude, as between themselves, from the political-offense exception to extradition. Specifically, Article 1 provides:

> For the purposes of extradition between Contracting States, none of the following offences shall be regarded as a political offence or as an offence connected with a political offence or as an offence inspired by political motives:
>
>   (a) an offence within the scope of the Convention for the Suppression of Unlawful Seizure of Aircraft, signed at The Hague on 16 December 1970;
>
>   (b) an offence within the scope of the Convention for the Suppression of Unlawful Acts against the Safety of Civil Aviation, signed at Montreal on 23 September 1971;
>
>   (c) a serious offence involving an attack against the life, physical integrity or liberty of internationally protected persons, including diplomatic agents;
>
>   (d) an offence involving kidnapping, the taking of a hostage or serious unlawful detention;

(e) an offence involving the use of a bomb, grenade, rocket, automatic firearm or letter or parcel bomb if this use endangers persons;

(f) an attempt to commit any of the foregoing offences or participation as an accomplice of a person who commits or attempts to commit such an offence.

The European Convention is not itself an extradition agreement—it merely modifies existing bilateral and multilateral extradition arrangements among states parties to it. In attempting to include a variety of common crimes as well as "terrorism" notwithstanding their political overtones, the convention may have attempted too much. A number of states have, upon signing or ratifying the convention, reserved the right to refuse to extradite for an offense they consider political.

The Dublin Agreement, sponsored by the European Economic Community (EEC), is, as its full title suggests, simply a mechanism for promoting the application of the European Convention among member states of the EEC.[31] It contains no provisions relevant to definition of covered acts.

Bilateral

No bilateral agreement contains a definition of international terrorism. Several recently concluded U.S. extradition treaties, however, expressly prohibit the application of the political-offense exception to those crimes covered by the global antiterrorist conventions.[32] Moreover, the recently concluded U.S.-UK Supplementary Extradition Treaty[33] is directed primarily against terrorist acts committed by the Irish Republican Army in Northern Ireland. This highly controversial agreement follows the European Convention on the Suppression of Terrorism in setting forth an expansive list of crimes as to which the political-offense exception is inapplicable.

National

Countries Other Than the United States. At the national level most states have approached terrorism the same way they have at the international level—by refraining from defining terrorism in their criminal statutes and instead prosecuting terrorist crimes under statutes covering murder, kidnapping, explosives, and so on. Moreover, states adopting the antiterrorist conventions have passed implementing legislation to allow them to fulfill their obligation under these conventions to prosecute alleged offenders if they choose not to extradite. This implementing legislation, however, tends not to refer specifically to "terrorism."

Although a few states have adopted antiterrorist statutes, these are exceptions and are often highly controversial. Even when the term "terrorism" is expressly used in such national legislation, it is not always defined.

New Zealand has defined "terrorism" under its national law, but not for the purpose of prosecuting criminal acts. Rather, the term is defined in the Immigration Amendment Act of 1978[34] for the purpose of allowing the deportation of persons committing offenses or threatening national security. Under this law an "act of terrorism" is defined as follows:

> For the purposes of subsection (3) of this section, the term "act of terrorism" means—
>
> (a) Any act that involves the taking of human life, or threatening to take human life, or the wilful or reckless endangering of human life, carried out for the purpose of furthering an ideological aim;
>
> (b) Any act involving any explosive or incendiary device causing or likely to cause the destruction of or serious damage to any premises, building, installation, vehicle, or vessel, or property of a kind referred to in any of sections 298 to 304, except subsection (3) of section 298, of the Crimes Act 1961, carried out for the purpose of furthering an ideological aim;
>
> (c) Any act that constitutes, or that would, if committed in New Zealand, constitute, an offence against any of the provisions of the Aviation Crimes Act 1972;—
>
> and includes the planning of any such act.[35]

New Zealand has also passed legislation allowing it to fulfill its obligations under the antiterrorist conventions.

Under British legislation, directed primarily at the situation in Northern Ireland, "terrorism" is broadly defined as "the use of violence for political ends, and includes any use of violence for the purpose of putting the public or any section of the public in fear."[36]

The United Kingdom has also implemented the antiterrorist conventions through the passage of legislation.

Perhaps the most sweeping definition of terrorism in national legislation is that found in South Africa's Internal Security Act of 1982:

> (1) Any person who with intent to—
>   (a) overthrow or endanger the State authority in the Republic;
>   (b) achieve, bring about or promote any constitutional, political, industrial, social or economic aim or change in the Republic;
>   (c) induce the Government of the Republic to do or to abstain from doing any act or to adopt or to abandon a particular standpoint; or
>   (d) put in fear or demoralize the general public, a particular population group or the inhabitants of a particular area in the Republic, or to induce the said public or such population group or inhabitants to do or to abstain from doing any act,
>
> in the Republic or elsewhere—
>
>   (i) commits an act of violence or threatens or attempts to do so;
>   (ii) performs any act which is aimed at causing, bringing about, promoting or contributing towards such act or threat of violence, or attempts, consents or takes any steps to perform such act;
>   (iii) conspires with any other person to commit, bring about or perform any act or threat referred to in paragraph (i) or act referred to in paragraph (ii), or to aid in the commission, bringing about or performance thereof; or
>   (iv) incites, instigates, commands, aids, advises, encourages or procures any other person to commit, bring about or perform such act or threat, shall be guilty of the offence of terrorism and liable on conviction to the penalties provided for by law for the offence of treason.[37]

Coupled with this definition of terrorism are equally expansive definitions of "subversion" and "sabotage."

By contrast, Pakistan has passed legislation directed toward the "suppression of terrorist activities" that nowhere defines terrorism.[38] The approach, like that of the European Convention on the Suppression of Terrorism, is to refer to a schedule of specific offenses covered by the act, such as the use of explosives.

The Republic of Ireland has extended its criminal jurisdiction to encompass the commission of certain offenses in Northern Ireland that could be described as terrorist.[39] Here, however, the term "terrorism" nowhere appears in the legislation, nor is it defined. The law extends to such offenses as carrying a firearm with criminal intent or using explosives.

The United States. In the United States there have been governmental attempts to define terrorism at both the state and the federal level. A number of states have adopted antiterrorist legislation,[40] most of which consists of so-called terroristic-threat statutes. Few of these laws define terrorism; the California Penal Code is an exception. In it, a terrorist is defined as follows:

Any person who willfully threatens to commit a crime which will result in death or great bodily injury to another person, with intent to terrorize another or with reckless disregard of the risk of terrorizing another, and who thereby either:

(a) Causes another person reasonably to be in sustained fear for his or her or their immediate family's safety;

(b) Causes the evacuation of a building, place of assembly, or facility used in public transportation;

(c) Interferes with essential public services; or

(d) Otherwise causes serious disruption of public activities, is guilty of a felony and shall be punished by imprisonment in the state prison.
. . .

As used in this title, "terrorize" means to create a climate of fear and intimidation by means of threats or violent action causing sustained fear for personal safety in order to achieve social or political goals.[41]

Most states have avoided including phrases like "in order to achieve social or political goals" in their legislation because they wish to avoid complicating the legal issue of intent by requiring a particular motive as an essential element of the crime. As we shall see, this problem has arisen also at the federal level.

The basic distinction at the federal level is between definitions used for administrative purposes—for example, by the Department of State, the CIA, or the FBI—and those contained in federal legislation. The executive branch's definition of international terrorism has appeared in several forms in recent years. According to

Robert Oakley, formerly ambassador-at-large for counterterrorism, the executive branch currently defines "international terrorism" as the "premeditated use of violence against noncombatant targets for political purposes, involving citizens or territory of more than one country."[42]

Most federal legislation that deals with international terrorism does not define the term. For example, several laws now provide for sanctions of various kinds against foreign countries that support international terrorism.[43] The absence of a definition provides the executive branch with maximum flexibility in determining whether sanctions will be applied against a particular country.

There have been attempts to limit this flexibility. In 1978 Congress held extensive hearings on an Act to Combat International Terrorism,[44] which would have required the president to impose certain sanctions against countries that support it. The bill defined "international terrorism" to include any act designated under the anti-terrorist conventions then in force, as well as "any other unlawful act which results in the death, bodily harm, or forcible deprivation of liberty to any person, or in the violent destruction of property, or an attempt or credible threat to commit any such act," when the act was "intended to damage or threaten the interests of or obtain concessions from a state or an international organization."[45] To be "international" the act had to be committed under transnational circumstances similar to those specified in the 1972 U.S. draft convention. Like it, the 1978 bill would have excluded attacks against the military from the definition's coverage.

Although the 1978 bill never became law, in that same year Congress enacted the first (and as yet only) federal statutory definition of "terrorism." The Foreign Intelligence Surveillance Act (FISA) provides in pertinent part:

International terrorism means activities that—

(1) involve violent acts or acts dangerous to human life that are a violation of the criminal laws of the United States or of any State, or that would be a criminal violation if committed within the jurisdiction of the United States or any State;

(2) appear to be intended—

(A) to intimidate or coerce a civilian population;

(B) to influence the policy of a government by intimidation or coercion; or

(C) to affect the conduct of a government by assassination or kidnapping; and

(3) occur totally outside the United States, or transcend national boundaries in terms of the means by which they are accomplished, the persons they appear intended to coerce or intimidate, or the locale in which their perpetrators operate or seek asylum.[46]

Unlike the proposed Act to Combat International Terrorism, FISA does not deal with the imposition of sanctions; it serves only as a predicate for the application of the electronic surveillance permitted by the act under certain circumstances.

An abbreviated version of the FISA definition appears in the definition of "act of terrorism" employed in the U.S. attorney general's statutory authority to grant rewards to persons supplying information about acts of terrorism.[47] Numerous other antiterrorism bills introduced in Congress have used the FISA definition (or a close approximation); it was incorporated by reference into S. 1429, the Terrorist Prosecution Act of 1985.[48]

The antiterrorism penal legislation that finally emerged from the 99th Congress, however, did not define international terrorism. The Omnibus Diplomatic Security and Antiterrorism Act of 1986 provides U.S. criminal jurisdiction over the killing of, or an act of physical violence with intent to cause serious bodily injury to or that results in such injury to, a U.S. national outside the United States.[49] Although the relevant chapter of the act is entitled Extra-Territorial Jurisdiction Over Terrorist Acts Abroad Against United States Nationals, there is no requirement that the killing or violent act include the traditional elements of a terrorist act. Instead the legislation incorporates the element of terrorism as a limitation on prosecutorial discretion:

(e) LIMITATION ON PROSECUTION.—No prosecution for any offense described in this section shall be undertaken by the United States except on written certification of the Attorney General or the highest ranking subordinate of the Attorney General with responsibility for criminal prosecutions that, in the judgment of the certifying official, such offense was intended to coerce, intimidate, or retaliate against a government or a civilian population.

The conference report on the act makes clear that the certification of the attorney general or his designate is final and not subject to judicial review.[50] The conference report also clarifies the meaning of the term "civilian population" by noting that it "includes a general population as well as other specific identifiable segments of society such as the membership of a religious faith or of a particular nationality."[51] It is not necessary that either the targeted government or the civilian population be that of the United States.

The Omnibus Diplomatic Security and Antiterrorism Act of 1986 dropped any reference to terrorism as an element of the offense for reasons in themselves enlightening. These have been nicely summarized by Geoffrey Levitt, an attorney in the Office of the Legal Adviser, Department of State, who worked on the act. Levitt first suggests that the political-intent element characteristic of a "generic" definition of terrorism is inherently vague and then states:

> In the U.S. legal context, this flaw poses fundamental constitutional problems. The due process clause requires that criminal statutes "give a person of ordinary intelligence fair warning that his contemplated conduct is forbidden by the statute." When first amendment concerns are also involved, as they would of necessity be in any statute that included a politically oriented intent element, this requirement has even greater force. Even were such problems somehow resolved, the breadth of a generic intent element would severely complicate the task of prosecutors, who would be required to prove beyond a reasonable doubt the presence of a particular political motivation. Consequently, this would leave the Government open to accusations of selective prosecution based on the political views of defendants. A separate but substantial problem would be the likely absence of a similar intent element in the penal law of extradition treaty partners, thus removing the factor of dual criminality, a prerequisite to extradition—and one must wonder what the point would be of an international terrorism offense for which the United States could not successfully request the extradition of suspected offenders.[52]

Private Sector Definitions

Attempting to define international terrorism has been a popular activity among academics and other persons in the private sector. Accordingly, the discussion of these attempts will be highly selective, focusing on the proposals that are, in my opinion, the most innovative or represent the views of noteworthy private institutions.

Professor Jordan Paust has described terrorism as "the purposive use of violence or the threat of violence by the perpetrators against an instrumental target in order to communicate to a primary target a threat of future violence so as to coerce the primary target into behavior or attitudes through intense fear or anxiety in connection with a demanded (political) outcome."[53] Instrumental and primary targets might be the same person or groups of persons; Paust cites as an example an attack on a military headquarters in order to instill terror or intense anxiety in its military elite. He notes further that "the instrumental target need not be a person since attacks on power stations can produce a terror outcome in the civilian population of the community dependent upon the station for electricity."[54] So defined, international terrorism might include—assuming the presence of a terrorizing outcome, a political goal, and an international dimension—the explosion of bombs in the marketplace, the taking of hostages, attacks on international businesspersons and diplomats, the hijacking of airplanes, the threat to use nuclear materials or chemical and biological weapons, and attacks on energy resources such as pipelines, offshore rigs, and tankers carrying oil or natural gas.

Grant Wardlaw, an Australian scholar, also has advanced a thought-provoking definition. One of Wardlaw's primary goals is to "spell out clearly that terrorism may be used by both insurgents and incumbent regimes," and he thus proposes the following working definition of political terrorism:

> [T]he use, or threat of use, of violence by an individual or a group, whether acting for or in opposition to established authority, when such action is designed to create extreme anxiety and/or fear-inducing effects in a target group larger than the immediate victims with the purpose of coercing that group into acceding to the political demands of the perpetrators.[55]

Wardlaw further points out that this definition reflects his conviction that terrorism is usually not "mindless, senseless or wanton." On the contrary, he states, for the terrorist, terrorism is a means to an end. It has firm goals in mind, however perverse these may seem to the terrorist's adversaries.

Professors Thomas Franck and Bert Lockwood, in a 1974 article,[56] did not propose a definition of international terrorism, but did raise some crucial interpretational issues about the term. These included whether the definition should be limited to individuals or groups of private actors or should include governments as well; the range of acts that should be covered; how to distinguish internationally cognizable acts of terrorism from acts properly left to national disposition; whether motive as well as intent should be included in defining the crime; and what range of victims should be covered.

A 1986 policy paper by the Atlantic Council defines terrorism as "politically motivated violence—including assassination, kidnapping, hostage-taking, theft, sabotage, extortion, and intimidation—conducted against governmental, civilian, or private sector targets by subnational groups or state agents not constrained by the rules of law."[57] The paper suggests that this definition "differs only in detail from the definition used by the State Department, which characterizes terrorism as 'premeditated, politically motivated violence perpetrated against noncombatant targets by subnational groups or clandestine state agents.' Presumably the State Department definition would not exclude military personnel not engaged in actual combat."[58]

Perhaps the most thoughtful definition yet produced by a private organization—of interest because it reflects the views of scholars and practitioners of international law from different countries and legal systems—is set forth in a report of the Committee on International Terrorism of the International Law Association.[59] The committee's report begins with a statement of principle: "Certain acts are so reprehensible that they are of concern to the international community, whether they are perpetrated in time of peace or war, irrespective of the justice of the cause which the perpetrators pursue, and regardless of political motivation. All such acts must be suppressed."[60] The report then sets forth a working definition and an explanation:

Working Definition:
The acts referred to in the Statement of Principle include acts defined as offenses of international significance in treaties as well as

acts of international terrorism. Acts of international terrorism include but are not limited to atrocities, wanton killing, hostage taking, hijacking, extortion, or torture committed or threatened to be committed whether in peacetime or in wartime for political purposes provided that an international element is involved. An act of terrorism is deemed to have an international element when the offense is committed within the jurisdiction of one country.

(a) against any foreign government or international organization, or any representative thereof; or

(b) against any national of a foreign country because he is a national of a foreign country; or

(c) by a person who crosses an international frontier into another country from which his extradition is requested.

EXPLANATION. To be classified as "international terrorism" for the purposes of applying the rules of law set out here, an act must be so reprehensible or so disruptive of the fabric of society that no motivation or political subordination can excuse it. The acts listed here as illustrative include acts which violate all known municipal criminal law codes and which, if done in wartime, would seem to be violations of the laws of war. In the absence of an international element, all these acts are properly handled by each state for itself. When an international element is involved, the suppression of these and similar acts becomes a matter of international concern. Three situations are envisaged in which the international element must be deemed to exist.[61]

Defining International Terrorism:
A Way Out of the Quagmire

As the preceding discussion demonstrates, a generally acceptable definition of international terrorism has been a will-o'-the-wisp. Levitt has suggested that the search for a legal definition of terrorism "in some ways resembles the quest for the Holy Grail"[62]—surely an apt description of the process at the international level. Even at the national level there have been few examples of general legislative definitions.

Perhaps it is time to adopt a functional approach, allowing the definition of international terrorism to vary depending upon the purpose the definition is intended to serve. In some situations, however, defining international terrorism may undermine efforts to develop a collective response to it.

A look at the primary components of most definitions of terrorism will help us to understand why it has proven impossible to reach agreement in the United Nations and other international organizations. These definitions almost invariably include a political purpose or motivation behind the violent act and a government as the primary target, factors that serve to distinguish terrorism from violent acts classified as common crimes. The political purpose of the violent act is to influence the policy of a government by intimidation or coercion. These same factors, however, may lead some governments to be not only unwilling to criminalize such behavior but prone actively to support it.

The African National Congress and South Africa offer an example. South Africa today is truly an international pariah—its apartheid practices are condemned by all decent-minded people. The ANC, in a "war of national liberation," has the announced goal of overthrowing the white government of South Africa and installing a black one in its place, a policy of revolutionary violence endorsed by the overwhelming majority of member states of the United Nations. But the ANC's policy is not supported by the Western developed states, and hence any formula defining terrorism as politically motivated violence intended to influence the policy of a government by intimidation or coercion has no chance of success in the United Nations. Indeed, under such an expansive standard many governments, including perhaps that of the United States, could be charged with engaging in "terrorist" behavior from time to time.

Levitt has neatly pinpointed the primary difficulties in reaching agreement on a generic definition of international terrorism at the United Nations:

Put simply, governments that have a strong political stake in the promotion of "national liberation movements" are loath to subscribe to a definition of terrorism that would criminalize broad areas of conduct habitually resorted to by such groups; and on the other end of the spectrum, governments against which these groups' violent activities are directed are obviously reluctant to subscribe to a definition that would criminalize their own use of force in response to such activities or otherwise.[63]

The record at the United Nations strongly supports these assertions.

It is important to recognize that support for wars of national liberation and repressive responses by target governments themselves raise profound issues of law and morality—issues that deserve a great deal more analysis than they have received to date. But clear analysis of these issues is hindered rather than helped by treating them as part of the problem of terrorism. Instead the legality of state support of wars of national liberation should be tested under the norms of the United Nations Charter regarding the threat or use of force. Government reactions to state support that involve the use or threat of force should be tested under the same UN Charter norms. Repressive responses against individuals by target governments should be tested under international human rights law.

Even though the United Nations has been successful in adopting certain legal measures—some described earlier, such as the conventions against hijacking of or sabotage against civil aviation, attacks on internationally protected persons, hostage taking, and theft of nuclear material used for civilian purposes—it has not resolved the problem of defining international terrorism. The UN has avoided the issue, focusing instead on acts that should be regarded as impermissible under any circumstances and therefore subject to vigorous international cooperation toward their suppression and punishment. Perhaps the time has come for the United States and like-minded states to expressly recognize the futility of attempting to define terrorism in the United Nations and to advance proposals for legal measures that would combat major forms of terrorist acts currently neglected by international treaty law—for example, the deliberate targeting, by bombs or other means, of civilians, and theft of nuclear material used for military purposes.[64]

A more precise focus on those acts that deserve the world community's condemnation under any circumstances also would help member states of the United Nations to carry out the recommendations of Resolution 40/61.[65] In that resolution the General Assembly, *inter alia*, "[u]*nequivocally condemns*, as criminal, all acts, methods and practices of terrorism wherever and by whomever committed, including those which jeopardize friendly relations among States and their security"; invites states "[t]o take all appropriate measures at the national level . . . such as the harmonization of domestic legislation with existing international conventions, the fulfillment of assumed international obligations, and the prevention of the preparation and organization in their respective territories of acts directed against other States"; calls upon states "to fulfill their obligations under international law to refrain from organizing, instigating, assisting or participating in terrorist acts in other States, or acquiescing in activities within their territory directed towards the commission of such acts"; appeals to all states to become parties to the existing antiterrorist conventions and urges all states "to cooperate with one another more closely, especially through the exchange of relevant information concerning the prevention and combatting of terrorism, apprehension and prosecution or extradition of the perpetrators of such acts, the conclusion of special treaties and/or the incorporation into appropriate bilateral treaties of special clauses, in particular regarding the extradition or prosecution of terrorists."

If states are to harmonize their domestic legislation with respect to terrorism, and if they are to cooperate more effectively in the extradition or prosecution of terrorists, the focus will have to be on a narrow spectrum of acts that most states regard as impermissible under all circumstances. In a less fractious United Nations, it might be possible to reach agreement on a wide-ranging generic definition of international terrorism—although even a harmonious atmosphere is no guarantee, considering the difficulties of reaching agreement on such a definition in Europe and in the United States. In any event, given the intractable conceptual and political differences among states on this issue, a UN definition would be so ambiguous as to provide a further basis for dispute and invective. Accordingly, whenever possible, use of the term "terrorism" in United Nations debates and negotiations should be avoided.

To be sure, a focus on particular acts rather than on a generic definition of terrorism is not cost-free. However, the cost may be more theoretical than real. As Levitt has pointed out in commenting on what he calls the "inductive method" of approaching international terrorism:

This is not to say that—particularly in the international setting—the inductive approach represents the best of all possible worlds, or that the deductive approach can be discarded without sacrifice. The problem with the inductive method, from the viewpoint of counter-terrorism, is its lack of specific focus on terrorism per se. Not all hijackings, sabotages, attacks on diplomats, or even hostage-takings are "terrorist"; such acts may be done for personal or pecuniary reasons or simply out of insanity. The international legal instruments that address these acts are thus in a sense "overbroad" themselves: the attack of an enraged spouse on a philandering diplomat who has been cheating with the former's partner is hardly of the same international significance as the assassination of the Ambassador by militant separatists. Such diffuseness tends to undermine the moral and political force of these instruments as a counter-terrorism measure. This feature is also, however, precisely what renders the instruments facially neutral and thereby permits them to be concluded in the first place by a disparate and fractious international community. In the construction of anti-terrorist legal mechanisms, as in so many other enterprises, the best may indeed be the enemy of the good.[66]

The wide-ranging FISA definition has been challenged as being overbroad under the First Amendment to the Constitution and as giving the judiciary unconstitutionally broad authority to make foreign policy. These challenges have not been successful.[67] Moreover, the FISA definition seems appropriate to serve the functions of the statute. FISA does not seek to criminalize international terrorism or to compel a certain U.S. response to it by way of sanction; it only authorizes electronic surveillance, within strict limits, of certain persons and groups suspected of engaging in or planning acts of international terrorism. The goal is to obtain intelligence information, and for this purpose a narrow definition of international terrorism would be dysfunctional.

For the purpose of prosecuting and punishing international terrorists, however, the FISA type of definition appears clearly dysfunctional, for reasons previously discussed: In sum, the broad FISA definition would increase the difficulty of obtaining extradition of terrorists because of the dual criminality and political-offense exception provisions contained in most U.S. extradition treaties, and would also enhance the problems of prosecutors faced with proving the requisite intent or political motivation of an alleged offender.

It is too early to tell how successful the innovative device contained in the Omnibus and Diplomatic Security and Antiterrorism Act of 1986 will prove in practice. Use of an abbreviated version of the

FISA definition as a limitation on prosecution of extraterritorial crimes, however, is important to support the legality under international law of a prosecution under the act. Absent a FISA-style limitation on prosecution, the international legal basis for prosecution would be the passive personality principle—the nationality of the victim—which is highly controversial and has not traditionally enjoyed the support of the United States.[68] By contrast, if prosecution is limited to situations in which the victim is a U.S. national *and* the offense was "intended to coerce, intimidate, or retaliate against a government or a civilian population," a good argument can be made that prosecution would be supported by the protective principle and—somewhat less convincingly—the universality principle of international criminal jurisdiction. Under the protective principle, a state is entitled to exercise jurisdiction over acts perpetrated abroad if they have a potentially adverse effect upon its security or the operation of its government functions. Acts fitting within the FISA type of definition necessarily impact on national security and interfere with the government's conduct of foreign relations.[69] The universality principle of jurisdiction may be a more questionable basis for prosecution because, as we have seen, the world community has not agreed on a definition of international terrorism. But the universality principle may lend some support to prosecution when the attack deliberately targets the civilian population—such attacks are clearly prohibited under the law of armed conflict, and there is increasing support for the proposition that they are illegal as well in situations outside of armed conflict.[70]

A Functional Definition in Situations Involving State Sponsorship or Support

The primary focus of this study is not the prosecution and punishment of terrorists but an exploration of measures that might be effective against states that sponsor or support terrorism. For reasons that should be apparent by now, the FISA type of definition would seem inappropriate for identifying those states that sponsor or support international terrorism and inducing them to cease their behavior. Terrorism instead should be defined as those acts already covered by the antiterrorist conventions or those identified by a substantial majority of the world community as impermissible under any circumstances. The need for a narrow definition will be further demonstrated in the next chapter, where we turn to a consideration of the elusive concepts of "state support" and "state sponsorship."

Notes

1. Laqueur, *Reflections on Terrorism*, 64 FOREIGN AFF. 86, 88 (1986).

2. Baxter, *A Skeptical Look at the Concept of Terrorism*, 7 AKRON L. REV. 380 (1974).

3. A. SEBOUL, THE FRENCH REVOLUTION, 1780–1799, at 385 (1975).

4. R. FRIEDLANDER, TERROR VIOLENCE, 7–8 (1983).

5. *Id.* at 30.

6. *Id.* at 31.

7. Franck & Lockwood, *Preliminary Thoughts Towards an International Convention on Terrorism*, 68 AM. J. INT'L L. 69, 73, fn. 23 (1974).

8. The text of the convention may be most conveniently found in 1 R. FRIEDLANDER, TERRORISM 253 (1979).

9. Article 1(2) of the convention.

10. Franck & Lockwood, *supra* note 7, at 70.

11. 9 U.N. GAOR, Supp. 9, at 11–12, UN Doc. A/2693 (1972).

12. Article 2(5) of the draft code.

13. Draft Convention for the Prevention and Punishment of Certain Acts of International Terrorism (Draft Convention to Prevent the Spread of Terrorist Violence), UN Doc. A/C.6/L.850 (1972). The text of the convention may also be found in R. FRIEDLANDER, TERRORISM, *supra* note 8, at 487.

14. *See* Murphy, *United Nations Proposals on the Control and Repression of Terrorism*, M. C. BASSIOUNI (ed.), INTERNATIONAL TERRORISM AND POLITICAL CRIMES 493, 499 (1975).

15. *Id.*

16. *Id.* at 501.

17. Convention on Offenses and Certain Other Acts Committed on Board Aircraft, Sept. 14, 1963, 20 U.S.T. 2941, T.I.A.S. No. 6768, 704 U.N.T.S. 219; Convention for Suppression of Unlawful Seizure of Aircraft, Dec. 16, 1970, 22 U.S.T. 1641, T.I.A.S. No. 7192, 860 U.N.T.S. 105, *reprinted in* 10 I.L.M. 133 (1971).

18. Convention for Suppression of Unlawful Acts Against the Safety of Civil Aviation, Sept. 23, 1971, 24 U.S.T. 565, T.I.A.S. No. 7570, 974 U.N.T.S. 177, *reprinted in* 10 I.L.M. 1151 (1971).

19. On February 24, 1988, an International Civil Aviation Organization Conference held in Montreal adopted a protocol to the Montreal Convention—the Convention for the Suppression of Unlawful Acts of Violence at Airports Serving International Civil Aviation—that extends the provisions of the Montreal Convention to cover sabotage and other unlawful acts that take place in airports. Under this protocol, attacks such as those that occurred at the Rome and Vienna airports in 1985 would be covered. For the text of the convention, see 27 I.L.M. 627 (1988).

20. Convention on Prevention and Punishment of Crimes Against Internationally Protected Persons, Including Diplomatic Agents, Dec. 14, 1973, 28 U.S.T. 1975, T.I.A.S. No. 8532, 1035 U.N.T.S. 167.

21. International Convention Against the Taking of Hostages, 34 U.N. GAOR Supp. (No. 39) at 23, U.N. Doc. A/34/39 (1979), *reprinted in* 18 I.L.M. 1456 (1979).

22. Convention on the Physical Protection of Nuclear Materials, *opened for signature* Mar. 3, 1980, ____U.S.T. ____, T.I.A.S. No. ____, ____U.N.T.S. ____, *reprinted in* 18 I.L.M. 1419 (1979).

23. On March 10, 1988, the International Maritime Organization adopted a Convention for the Suppression of Unlawful Acts Against the Safety of Maritime Navigation as well as a Protocol for the Suppression of Unlawful Acts Against the Safety of Fixed Platforms Located on the Continental Shelf. The texts of these documents may be found in 27 I.L.M. 672, 685 (1988).

24. G.A. Res. 40/61, 40 U.N. GAOR Supp. (No. 53) at 301, UN Doc. A/40/53 (1985), *reprinted in* 25 I.L.M. 239 (1986).

25. N.Y. Times, Dec. 10, 1985, at A4, col. 1.

26. The Declaration on Principles of International Law Concerning Friendly Relations and Co-operation Among States in Accordance with the Charter of the United Nations, Oct. 24, 1970, G.A. Res. 2625, 25 U.N. GAOR Supp. (No. 28) at 121, U.N. Doc. A/8028 (1970) provides: "Every State has the duty to refrain from organizing, instigating, assisting or participating in acts of civil strife or terrorist acts in another State or acquiescing in organized activities within its territory directed towards the commission of such acts."

27. Resolution A/Res/42/22, adopted on November 18, 1987.

28. Convention to Prevent and Punish the Acts of Terrorism Taking the Form of Crimes Against Persons and Related Extortion That Are of International Significance, Feb. 2, 1971, 27 U.S.T. 3949, T.I.A.S. No. 8413, O.A.S.T.S. No. 37 at 6, O.A.S. Doc. OEA/Ser.A/17.

29. European Convention on the Suppression of Terrorism, *opened for signature* Jan. 27, 1977, 1978 Gr. Brit. T.S. No. 93 (Cmd. 7390), Europ. T.S. No. 90, *reprinted in* 15 I.L.M. 1272 (1976).

30. Agreement Concerning the Application of the European Convention on the Suppression of Terrorism Among the Member States, Dec. 4, 1979, 19 I.L.M. 325 (1980).

31. The Dublin Agreement seeks to do this in two ways: First, member states of the EEC accept the proposition that in extradition proceedings between member states, the European Convention will apply in full *even if* one or both of the states are not a party to it, or if one or both have made a political-offense reservation. Second, the agreement provides that signatories to the European Convention that have made such a reservation must declare whether they intend to utilize it. Also, states parties to the Dublin Agreement but not to the European Convention are required to indicate by declaration whether they wish to retain the political-offense reservation in extradition proceedings between EEC member states.

32. *See, e.g.,* Extradition Treaty, May 4, 1978, United States–Mexico, art. 5, para. 2(a), 31 U.S.T. 5059, 5064, T.I.A.S. No. 9656, at 4.

33. ____U.S.T. ____, T.I.A.S. No. ____. The final version of the treaty, which was revised in the course of proceedings before the Senate Committee on Foreign Relations, may be found at 132 CONG. REC. S9119–20 (daily ed. July 16, 1986). For a more extensive discussion of this treaty, *see* Murphy, *The Future of Multilateralism and Efforts to Combat International Terrorism,* 25 COLUM. J. TRANSNAT'L L. 35, 64–65, 77–79 (1986).

34. For discussion and the text of the act, *see* Y. ALEXANDER & A. NANES (eds.), LEGISLATIVE RESPONSES TO TERRORISM 117, 119 (1986).

35. *Id.* at 119.

36. Prevention of Terrorism (Temporary Provisions) Act 1984, section 14(1), *id.* at 261, 271.

37. Internal Security Act 1982, section 54(1), *id.* at 189, 202.

38. Suppression of Terrorist Activities (Special Courts) Act 1975, *id.* at 155.

39. Criminal Law (Jurisdiction) Act 1976, *id.* at 75.

40. For a discussion of this legislation, *see* Smith, *Antiterrorism Legislation in the United States: Problems and Implications,* 7 TERRORISM 213, 221 (1984).

41. California Penal Code, Title 11.5, 422, Y. ALEXANDER & A. NANES, *supra* note 34, at 308–09.

42. Oakley, *International Terrorism,* 65 FOREIGN AFF. 611 (1987).

43. For a listing of some examples of such legislation, *see* Levitt, *Is "Terrorism" Worth Defining?* 13 OHIO NORTHERN L. REV. 97, 113–14, fn. 72 (1986).

44. S. 2236, S. REP. NO. 908, 95th Cong., 2d Sess. 91 (1978).

45. *Id.* at § 3(a)(4).

46. Foreign Intelligence Surveillance Act of 1978, section 101(c), 50 U.S.C. § 1801(c).

47. 18 U.S.C.A. § 3077 (West 1985).

48. S. 1429, § 2321(c), in *Hearing on Bills to Authorize Prosecution of Terrorists and Others Who Attack U.S. Government Employees and Citizens Abroad Before the Subcommittee on Security and Terrorism, Senate Comm. on the Judiciary*, 99th Cong., 1st Sess. 36–37 (1986).

49. 18 U.S.C. § 2331(e).

50. H. REP. 783, 99th Cong., 1st Sess. 88 (1986).

51. *Id.*

52. Levitt, *supra* note 43, at 113.

53. Paust, *Terrorism and the International Law of War*, 64 MILITARY L. REV. 1, 3–4 (1974).

54. *Id.*

55. G. WARDLAW, POLITICAL TERRORISM 16 (1982).

56. Franck & Lockwood, *Preliminary Thoughts Towards an International Convention on Terrorism*, *supra* note 7, at 72–82.

57. THE ATLANTIC COUNCIL OF THE UNITED STATES, COMBATTING INTERNATIONAL TERRORISM: U.S.-ALLIED COOPERATION AND POLITICAL WILL 15 (1986).

58. *Id.*

59. INTERNATIONAL LAW ASSOCIATION, REPORT OF THE SIXTY-FIRST CONFERENCE 313 (1984).

60. *Id.* at 314.

61. *Id.* at 314–15.

62. Levitt, *supra* note 43, at 97.

63. *Id.* at 109.

64. For discussion of this gap in the law, *see* Murphy, *Cooperative International Arrangements: Prevention of Nuclear Terrorism and the Extradition and Prosecution of Terrorists*, PREVENTING NUCLEAR TERRORISM 360 (P. Leventhal & Y. Alexander, eds. 1987).

65. G.A. Res. 40/61, *supra* note 24.

66. Levitt, *supra* note 43, at 115.

67. *See* United States v. Mehahey, 553 F. Supp. 1180, 1196 (E.D.N.Y. 1982) *aff'd* 729 F.2d 1444 (2d Cir. 1983); United States v. Falvey, 540 F. Supp. 1306, 1314 (E.D.N.Y. 1982).

68. *See, e.g.*, RESTATEMENT (SECOND) OF THE FOREIGN RELATIONS LAW OF THE UNITED STATES, § 30(2) (1965). The Third Restatement is much more tentative on the legality of the passive personality principle under international law. RESTATEMENT (THIRD) OF THE FOREIGN RELATIONS LAW OF THE UNITED STATES, § 402(g) (1988).

69. *See* Testimony of Abraham D. Sofaer, *Hearing on Bills to Authorize Prosecution of Terrorists and Others Who Attack U.S. Government Employees and Citizens Abroad, supra* note 48, at 66, 67.

70. *See* INTERNATIONAL LAW ASSOCIATION, REPORT OF THE SIXTY-FIRST CONFERENCE, *supra* note 59, at 314–15.

2

"State Support" and "State Sponsorship" of International Terrorism: The Legal Framework

As suggested at the end of Chapter 1, the need for a narrow definition of international terrorism becomes particularly apparent when we turn to a consideration of the concepts of "state support" and "state sponsorship" of it. Specifically, failure to distinguish carefully between terrorism and other kinds of violence makes "state support" and "state sponsorship" so broad in scope as to make the terms unmanageable from an operational perspective.

Defining the Concepts

Defense Systems, Inc. (DSI), has suggested a number of ways in which state-sponsored terrorism differs from other forms of terrorism:

- Attacks are more lethal;
- The scope of operations is more sophisticated;
- The political consequences for the target government tend to be greater;
- Law enforcement is more difficult because terrorists are supported by the diplomatic assets and intelligence resources of states;
- Economic and political ties with state sponsors make some governments reluctant to join fully in the fight to combat it; and

- The variety of responses available to governments to combat it is greater.[1]

An important operational factor that arises when a state is involved in international terrorism—rather than in helping to combat it—is that the focus of attention shifts from the individual to an entity; the concern shifts from punishing the individual terrorists for their crimes to inducing states supporting them to cease such support. The matter thus becomes less a problem of criminal law and more one of public international law, especially norms regarding the maintenance of international peace and security.

DSI has identified the following twelve types of state involvement:

- *State Terrorism*, the most active type of involvement, includes the use of state intelligence operatives to carry out terrorist acts in foreign countries.
- *Direct Support* is comprised of two distinct elements: planning and guidance. Planning means that the state is directly involved in the development of programs of action (sets of objectives, assets to be used pursuing them and schedules) involving terrorism. These plans may be long-term (plans for terrorist campaigns or to develop a terrorist cadre in an insurgency situation) or short-term (plans for a single, immediate action). The distinguishing characteristic of planning is that it always involves specific combinations of mission, assets, and schedules. Guidance is more general and includes information on how programs of action can be developed. It involves interaction between government agents and terrorists (probably terrorist leaders), but does not involve an obligation or expectation of action.
- *Intelligence Support* to terrorists is the provision of information, but unlike Direct Support, implies no control over what the terrorists do with the information provided.
- *Training* to terrorists is divided into two categories: *Specialized Terrorist* and *Basic Military*. The former includes training in intelligence gathering, infiltration, surveillance, and the use of sophisticated communications equipment, explosives, or weapons. The latter consists of basic infantry training with standard weapons including physical conditioning, marksmanship, hand-to-hand combat, and small unit tactics.
- *Diplomatic Assets* includes providing passports, documents, and other forms of cover. In addition, it involves use of the privileges of

extraterritoriality to further terrorism, e.g., the use of embassy or consulate grounds for organization activities.

- Provision of *High Technology,* including nuclear, biological, chemical, and exotic weapons is a type of terrorism where state involvement is extremely important and perhaps essential.

- Provision of *Weapons and Explosives* (not high technology) is a frequent form of state involvement. *Logistics* support, including media equipment and equipment for communications and surveillance, may have a considerable impact on terrorist group capabilities.

- Provision of *Transportation* includes not 'only the actual turning over of vehicles, boats, and so forth to terrorists, but also allowing the use of national transportation agencies (airlines, and so forth) by terrorists.

- By permitting terrorists *Use of Territory* a country supporting terrorism knowingly allows terrorists to use or transit national territory to plan attacks, train, avoid extradition, and otherwise elude international legal processes. This does not include use of diplomatic facilities abroad (see *Diplomatic Assets*), nor does it imply provision of government resources to terrorists.

- *Financial Support* may be direct or indirect. For example, it includes both the benefits accrued from direct government participation in the drug trade or those from allowing the terrorists to deal in drugs themselves.

- *Tacit Support* implies foreknowledge and failure to act. For example: failing to warn a target state that it is about to be attacked, or to take steps to prevent such an attack when it emanates from home territory. Refusal to cooperate with foreign intelligence and police is also a form of tacit support.

- *Rhetorical Support* suggests specific statements or speeches by authoritative government figures that call for, express approval of, or endorse the use of terrorism. It also includes government facilitation or support of terrorist efforts to communicate with target populations (propaganda); for example, printing materials for use abroad, use of government studios for producing propaganda films, broadcasting interviews with or polemic statements by terrorist leaders, and helping to forge materials intended to harm target governments' interests or smear individuals in highly visible positions. Rhetorical Support also includes the use of government agents to suggest terrorism to dissident groups.[2]

It may be useful to break the DSI types of state involvement into two basic categories: state support and state sponsorship. The latter would include only those situations in which the state contributes active planning, direction, and control to terrorist operations. So defined, "state sponsorship" would be limited to the first two types in the DSI list: state terrorism and direct support.

The other types identified by DSI would fall into the general category of "state support." Several of these types deserve further comment. For example, DSI's distinction between "specialized terrorist" and "basic military" training for terrorists may be more apparent than real. The crucial distinction would seem to be not between the type of training provided but between the kinds of purposes for which the training is provided.

Provision of transportation is often a concession that a state may make to terrorists as a result of negotiations with them. Egypt providing a plane to the hijackers of the *Achille Lauro* in order to take them to safe haven is one recent example.

Permitting use of territory for terrorist purposes is expressly prohibited by the Declaration on Principles of International Law Concerning Friendly Relations and Co-operation Among States in Accordance with the Charter of the United Nations,[3] a General Assembly declaration widely regarded as an authoritative interpretation of the UN Charter. The declaration provides:

> Every State has the duty to refrain from organizing, instigating, assisting or participating in acts of civil strife or terrorist acts in another State or acquiescing in organized activities within its territory directed towards the commission of such acts, when the acts referred to in the present paragraph involve a threat or use of force.[4]

Financial support for terrorists is a subject that is receiving increasing attention. In particular, so-called narco-terrorism—the financing of terrorist activity by funds derived from the drug trade—has been much in the news.

Tacit support of terrorism raises the issue of whether such "sins of omission" violate any legal obligation owed by the supporting states to other states or to the world community as a whole. In some instances tacit support may violate an antiterrorist convention to which the state is party, but the more difficult issue is whether a state has violated a norm of customary international law. Relevant to this point are some of the statements of applicable rules of law, proposed by the International Law Association's Committee on International Terrorism and adopted by the association at its 1984 conference. The statement of principle and the statements of applicable rules provide:

Article 1   Statement of Principle

Certain acts are so reprehensible that they are of concern to the international community, whether they are perpetrated in time of peace or war, irrespective of the justice of the cause which the perpetrators pursue, and regardless of political motivation. All such acts must be suppressed.

. . .

Article 7   Aut Judicare Aut Dedere

States must try to extradite (aut judicare aut dedere) persons accused of acts of international terrorism. No state may refuse to try or extradite a person accused of an act of international terrorism, war crime, common crime which would be a war crime but for the absence of a legal status of belligerency, or a crime against humanity, on the basis of disagreement as to which of these legal categories properly applies to the situation.

Article 8   State Support for International Terrorism Forbidden

No state may afford support to a person or group engaged or preparing to engage in acts of international terrorism.

Article 9   Due Diligence Required

A state is legally obliged to exercise due diligence to prevent the commission of acts of international terrorism within its jurisdiction.

Article 10   International Communication and Transportation of Universal Legal Concern

Acts of international terrorism directed against the means of international communication or transportation which by treaty or international practice are open to international traffic, are of legal interest to all states. No state may legally refuse to participate in measures to safeguard those means from acts of international terrorism on the ground of lack of legal interest.

Article 11   Organs of Communication and Diplomatic and Consular Establishments of Universal Legal Concern

Acts of international terrorism directed against official organs of communication, including diplomatic and consular establishments, special missions, and the people engaged in maintaining them, are of legal interest to all states. No state may legally refuse to participate in measures to safeguard those organs and people from acts of international terrorism on the ground of lack of legal interest.

Article 12   Specially Dangerous or Poisonous Materials of Universal Legal Concern

Acts of international terrorism involving the possession, diversion or use of specially dangerous or poisonous materials contrary to applicable national law or treaty, particularly nuclear materials, psychotropic drugs, and any materials made the subject of the 1972 Convention on the Development, Production and Stockpiling of Bacteriological (Biological) Toxin Weapons and on their Destruction, are of legal concern to all states. No state may refuse to participate in measures to safeguard such materials on the ground of lack of legal interest.

Article 13   State Responsibility

Breach of any of these rules entails state responsibility.[5]

Perhaps the most innovative—and controversial—aspect of the association's resolution is its proposal that states have an obligation to take various affirmative steps to combat terrorism, even if they elect not to become a party to the antiterrorist conventions. Such an obligation, if accepted by states, would clearly establish the illegality of tacit support.

Rhetorical support of terrorism is a subject that deserves more attention than it has received to date, and we will return to this topic when we consider possible responses to state-supported terrorism. Express approval of terrorist acts may lend a substantial measure of assistance to the ideological warfare waged by terrorists and give them the publicity for their cause that they often crave. (It may also stimulate more attacks.) Perhaps the most striking recent example of rhetorical support is the Libyan government's statement approving the terrorist attacks at the Rome and Vienna airports.

State involvement that takes the form of sponsorship of terrorism may constitute the waging of secret or undeclared warfare against an adversary state. Some have claimed that because of the dangers of military escalation in today's world of high technology, this form of so-called low-intensity conflict is becoming increasingly prevalent. As defined by the United States Army, low-intensity conflict is:

a broad term describing political-military struggle short of conventional warfare between national armed forces, to achieve political, social, economic, or psychological objectives. It is often protracted and ranges from diplomatic, economic, and psycho-social pressures through terrorism to insurgent war. The military aspects of LIC are characterized by constraints on the level of violence, weaponry, and tactics. LIC includes such activities as demonstrations of forces, security assistance, peacekeeping, rescue operations, terrorism counteraction, special operations, and limited direct use of regular military forces.[6]

Others have warned against equating even state-sponsored terrorism with war. Jeffrey Simon, for example, has recently pointed out:

Even when states fund or guide terrorism, it remains a different type of conflict from war. Unlike conventional warfare and guerrilla insurgencies, terrorism is primarily an urban phenomenon carried out by small cells of individuals who rarely battle government troops. Most terrorist groups seek to create a climate of fear through seemingly indiscriminate acts of violence. Also, terrorism can be perpetrated by a lone person in protest to a specific government policy. American citizens and facilities are vulnerable to terrorist assaults worldwide. But not all of these incidents can be considered acts of war, or the United States would be at war at every incident. The problem of finding an appropriate military response further distances terrorism from warfare among nation-states. Deterrence, pre-emption, and retaliation take on new meanings when applied to terrorist groups. Deterrence rests heavily on rationality. But the rationality posited in how two governments react to each other's policies cannot be applied to terrorist groups that use suicide tactics. It is likewise difficult to deter an enemy whose objective is to activate an escalating cycle of violence. Identifying who perpetrated a given incident is often difficult, as is locating the terrorists' base of operations. Terrorists can move quickly from one location to another, making intelligence on their whereabouts outdated. They can merge easily into urban areas, thus ensuring that any retaliatory or pre-emptive attack will result in the death of innocent civilians.[7]

Regardless of which side to this dispute is correct, it should be noted that inflicting terror in the context of an armed conflict is prohibited by the laws of war. Examples of such terrorism include the killing of defenseless prisoners of war and the slaughter of civilian noncombatants. Also, as noted in Chapter 1, the working definition of international terrorism proposed by the International Law Association covers various impermissible acts "committed or threatened to be committed whether in peacetime or in wartime."

A Case History: The 1978 Act
to Combat International Terrorism

By far the most ambitious effort to come to grips with the problem of state support of international terrorism as a matter of federal legislation was the series of hearings and reports in 1978 on S. 2236, An Act to Combat International Terrorism.[8] These efforts, which lasted for months, had as their primary goal the establishment of certain reporting requirements, especially a list of states supporting international terrorism, and the mandatory imposition of economic sanctions against them.

As noted in the previous chapter, the act's definition of "international terrorism" included any act designated as an offense under the antiterrorist conventions. It also included "any other unlawful act which results in the death, bodily harm, or forcible deprivation of liberty to any person, or in the violent destruction of property, or an attempt or credible threat to commit any such act" (under certain transnational circumstances similar to those set forth in the 1972 U.S. Draft Convention for the Prevention and Punishment of Certain Acts of International Terrorism) if the act was "intended to damage or threaten the interests of or obtain concessions from a state or an international organization."[9] As I testified before the Senate Committee on Foreign Relations, this definition was both overinclusive and underinclusive.[10]

The proposed legislation specified in subsection 3(b) that "state support of international terrorism" would consist of any of the following acts when committed deliberately by a state:

(1) furnishing arms, explosives, or lethal substances to individuals, groups, or organizations with the likelihood that they will be used in the commission of any act of international terrorism;

(2) planning, directing, providing training for, or assisting in the execution of any act of international terrorism;

(3) providing direct financial support for the commission of any act of international terrorism;

(4) providing diplomatic facilities intended to aid or abet the commission of any act of international terrorism; or

(5) allowing the use of its territory as a sanctuary from extradition or prosecution for any act of international terrorism.[11]

The joint report of the Senate Committees on Foreign Relations and on Commerce, Science, and Transportation[12] explains why this definition is restrictive: The intent is to exclude a state that has no actual control over the activities terrorists may be conducting in its territory or that lacks the real ability to prevent these attacks.

The provision of subsection 3(b)(3)—that "direct financial support for the commission of any act of international terrorism" would constitute state support—was designed to cope with perhaps the most complex nuance in this area. Many states, including some friendly to the United States like Saudi Arabia, provide funding to "national liberation groups" such as the Palestine Liberation Organization. Although this money may be designated as meant for nonterrorist activities, such funds are fungible and may be diverted from "legitimate" uses—such as the care of refugees—to terrorism. The Committees on Foreign Relations and on Commerce, Science, and Transportation therefore suggested that the president, in deciding whether a state had provided direct financial support to international terrorism, should consider "a number of factors including the nature of the organization to which the money was given and the organization's purposes, the real intent of the giving state and whether the state should have known the money or a significant part of it would be misdirected."[13]

Arguably, subsection 3(b)(5) was too expansive in its coverage. In the context of any particular instance of international terrorism, issues might arise as to whether a state had granted impermissible sanctuary to a terrorist or had only exercised its right under international law to grant political asylum. Accordingly, in testimony before the Senate Foreign Relations Committee, I suggested this provision be amended to read:

(5) allowing the use of its territory as a sanctuary, in violation of international obligations to prosecute or extradite perpetrators of acts of international terrorism.[14]

The report of the Senate Committee on Governmental Affairs had this to say about the definition of state support of international terrorism:

> The committee's definition of state actions is intended to include the granting of asylum to perpetrators of international terrorism; the intervention to seek the release of imprisoned terrorists; the provision of logistical aid (such as communications), monetary support, documentation, transportation, safe sites, cover and diplomatic immunity or facilities to terrorists; the allowing of terrorists to conduct training on its territory, and the provision of government instructors; the provision of arms; the providing of operational intelligence on potential targets; the overt aiding of terrorists during an incident including guarding of hostages against escaping or being rescued by outside forces. In addition, state actions might include support which is more directive, such as the state selecting targets for terrorists and contributing to the planning of attacks; the use of government and intelligence agents in terrorist operations; the adoption of the terrorist group as an arm of the sponsoring governments.[15]

The report of the Senate Select Committee on Intelligence, however, highlighted some possible practical difficulties with the definition:

> The select committee was deeply concerned about the definition of "state support of international terrorism" as set forth in section 3(b) of the bill. It must be emphasized that, in determining whether the actions of a state meet the criteria of this definition, it would not be necessary to provide the sort of evidence which could obtain a guilty verdict in a court of law. It is not necessary to prove "beyond a reasonable doubt" that a state has supported terrorism. In particular, in proving that a state has acted "deliberately" or that it "intended" to aid or abet the commission of any act of international terrorism, reliance can be placed on circumstantial, as opposed to direct, evidence of the state's intention. Similarly, if a state supplies arms to a group which has carried out terrorist acts in the past, direct evidence would not be necessary to establish that the arms were given in the "likelihood" that they would be used in the commission of an act of international terrorism.
>
> The definition of "state support of international terrorism" is a key to implementing sections 5 and 6 which require the listing of, and the imposing of sanctions on, states which "have demonstrated

a pattern of support for acts of international terrorism." The drafters intended this definition to exclude from its coverage indirect or inadvertent support for acts of international terrorism or indiscriminate moral support for groups which espouse terrorist tactics.

In attempting, however, to restrict the applicability of the definition to those states which are directly and actively involved in the support of international terrorism, the definition imposes strict standards of proof that it may be very difficult for the intelligence community to meet. For example, the "deliberateness" of a state's actions will of necessity be judged from circumstantial evidence, often of fairly limited scope and low quality. There is little certainty that we would possess a source of intelligence with access to a state's leadership to tell us just what the leadership intended when it agreed to furnish arms, money, diplomatic facilities, et cetera; and if such a source did exist, it would of course be impossible to disclose publicly either its existence or any information it supplied which might suggest its existence.

Similarly, it will be difficult to establish the precise conditions under which arms, explosives, or lethal substances were furnished by a state to a terrorist group; consequently, the judgment of whether or not the "likelihood" existed that they would be used in the commission of a terrorist act would necessarily contain a subjective element.

The remaining clauses of the definition pose similar problems for the intelligence community. In each clause, state support is defined as providing a particular kind of support "for any act of international terrorism." If this is interpreted as requiring that the intelligence community demonstrate a direct connection between the actions of the state and a particular terrorist act, it may be that the available evidence will not be found equal to the task. Rather, the executive branch and Congress may only be able to obtain evidence that demonstrates a close connection between a state and a terrorist group but which may not illuminate the precise relationship between the state and the given terrorist act.

The American people and Congress have a right to know which states support individuals or groups who commit acts of international terrorism by furnishing arms, explosives or lethal substances, providing training, money, cover, or diplomatic facilities, or by allowing their territory to be used as a sanctuary. The intelligence community is capable of providing some information on those matters with reasonable regularity. Of less material concern to Congress and the American people, at least for the purposes of this bill, is detailed information about the precise routes by which arms and money reach terrorists, and about the precise relationship between the terrorists and those who provide training camps for them, those who supply passports, and those who let them cross their countries' borders. The intelligence community often cannot provide such information.

The inherent subjectivity of the determinations which are required by the definition of state support has led some members of the select committee to fear that the determinations will be influenced unduly by foreign policy concerns independent of the available evidence. This development conceivably could lead to an arbitrary application of the sanctions and would deprive the list of moral authority. Since the public stigmatizing of a state as a supporter of international terrorism might be considered to be the strongest sanction available under the bill, it is of the utmost importance that the list not appear as being tailored to the particular foreign policy interests of a particular administration.[16]

Because of these concerns, some members of the select committee wished to eliminate the subjective elements of the definition and proposed the following substitute:

(b) "State support of international terrorism" shall consist of any of the following acts when committed by a state:
  (1) Furnishing arms, explosives, or lethal substances to any individual, group, or organization which engages in acts of international terrorism;
  (2) Directing, providing training for, or assisting any individual, group, or organization which plans or executes any act of international terrorism;
  (3) Providing financial support for any individual, group, or organization which plans or executes any act of international terrorism;
  (4) Providing diplomatic facilities which aid or abet the commission of any act of international terrorism; or
  (5) Failing to permit the extradition or prosecution of any individual within its territory who has committed any act of international terrorism.[17]

Other committee members favored the original definition, and the select committee decided not to recommend a change. Although the 1978 Act to Combat International Terrorism never became law, many of the issues raised in the hearings and reports on this draft legislation remain as difficult to resolve today as they were in 1978. These will be considered in later chapters.

A Functional Approach to State Support of International Terrorism

The definition of state support of international terrorism set forth in the proposed 1978 legislation just described was primarily designed to give guidance to the executive branch in its efforts to compile a list of states supporting international terrorism and against whom it should apply economic sanctions. Consequently, the definition was drawn narrowly in an attempt to avoid encompassing countries friendly to the United States. The purpose of defining state support of international terrorism for this study, however, is not so circumscribed. Here the goal is to gain an impression of the breadth and magnitude of the problem in order to evaluate what responses might be most effective and in accordance with law and policy. For example, economic sanctions—or even the use of military force—might be an appropriate response to a state engaged in the active sponsorship of international terrorism but clearly inappropriate for those states merely lending tacit support. Likewise, quiet diplomacy or the bringing of international claims might be effective with respect to a state lending tacit support and ineffective against a state sponsoring terrorism.

Thus different types of state support raise different issues and call for different types of response. Accordingly, this book will employ the typology suggested by Defense Systems, Inc. (modified as appropriate), with the goal being to match each type of state support with the appropriate response(s).

Notes

1. Defense Systems, Inc., is a consulting firm located in McLean, Virginia, that does extensive work on international terrorism. DSI very kindly made available to me some typologies on state-sponsored terrorism developed by the firm, and I am grateful to Dr. Richard E. Hayes and Dewey Covington of DSI for having done so.

2. DSI developed these typologies for purposes of its own research projects, but they constitute an excellent framework for a discussion of legal aspects of state support of international terrorism.

3. Declaration on Principles of International Law Concerning Friendly Relations and Co-Operation Among States in Accordance with the Charter

of the United Nations, Oct. 24, 1970, G.A. Res. 2625, 25 U.N. GAOR Supp. (No. 28) at 121, U.N. Doc A/8028 (1970).

4. *Id.* at First Principle, Ninth Paragraph.

5. INTERNATIONAL LAW ASSOCIATION, REPORT OF THE SIXTY-FIRST CONFERENCE 6–8 (1984).

6. Quoted in R. CLINE & Y. ALEXANDER, TERRORISM AS STATE-SPONSORED WARFARE 39 (1986).

7. Simon, *Misunderstanding Terrorism,* 67 FOREIGN POL'Y 104, 112 (1987).

8. S. 2236, S. REP. NO. 908, 95th Cong., 2d Sess. 91 (1978).

9. *Id.* at § 3(a)(4)(i).

10. Hearing on S. 2236, before the Comm. on Foreign Relations, 95th Cong., 2d Sess. 79, 81–82 (1978).

11. S. 2236, *supra* note 8, at § 3(b).

12. S. REP. NO. 970, 95th Cong., 2d Sess. 15 (1978).

13. *Id.* at 4.

14. See Hearing on S. 2236, *supra* note 10, at 82.

15. S. REP. NO. 908, 95th Cong., 2d. Sess. 54 (1978).

16. S. REP. NO. 1079, 95th Cong., 2d Sess. 6–7 (1978).

17. *Id.* at 7.

3

Intelligence and State Support of International Terrorism

There is general agreement that the collection and use of intelligence are effective tools in combatting terrorism. Ideally, the gathering of intelligence serves a preventive role and enables law enforcement officials to intercept terrorists at an early stage, before they inflict injury on persons or property. This has proven, however, to be a difficult goal to accomplish even with respect to purely private acts of terrorism that lack the added complication of state involvement. Once a state decides to lend its support, the complications increase.

Problems often arise at the national level. In the United States, for example, there is evidence that constraints imposed on intelligence activities from 1975 to 1980 may have adversely affected the timing and availability of preventive intelligence to the extent that the proportion of cases in which violence or other crimes were prevented declined.[1] The restrictions came following revelations during the 1970s of a history of executive branch abuse of the intelligence services for partisan political purposes, which convinced many, including Congress, that the intelligence community required stricter supervision. In particular, the work of congressional investigatory committees highlighted the intrusive nature of electronic surveillance and led to the adoption of the Foreign Intelligence Surveillance Act (FISA).[2]

FISA permits the collection of intelligence by electronic surveillance of persons in the United States participating in or preparing for international terrorist activities, but surveillance requires a judicial warrant with certain limited exceptions. The act defines "foreign intelligence information" in part as "information that relates to, and if concerning a United States person, is necessary to, the ability of the United States to protect against . . . sabotage or international terrorism by a foreign power or an agent of a foreign power."[3]

One exception to the warrant requirement allows the president, through the attorney general, to authorize electronic surveillance for up to one year without a warrant if the attorney general certifies under oath that the surveillance will be directed exclusively at communications between foreign powers.[4] This surveillance must be conducted in such a way that there is no substantial likelihood that the communication intercepted will be one to which a U.S. citizen is a party, and it must be performed in accordance with minimization procedures spelled out in the statute.[5] A second exception permits electronic surveillance under certain emergency circumstances, but a warrant must be obtained within twenty-four hours after the surveillance is conducted.[6]

In the absence of one of the exceptions, a warrant must be obtained from one of seven district court judges specially designated by the chief justice of the United States to hear and approve applications for electronic surveillance anywhere in the United States.[7] Appeal from denial of an application may be taken to a three-judge panel selected by the chief justice from the district courts or the courts of appeal.[8]

Under FISA there are two types of court order, and hence two different forms of applications, depending upon whether the target of the electronic surveillance is an "official" foreign power (i.e., a foreign government, a faction of a foreign nation, or an entity openly acknowledged by a foreign government to be controlled by that government). For "nonofficial" foreign powers or agents (i.e., a group engaged in international terrorism, a foreign-based political organization, or an entity directed or controlled by a foreign government), each application for an order must include the name of the federal officer making the application; a statement showing that the president has delegated authority to the attorney general to approve such applications and that the attorney general did approve the application; the identity or a description of the target; and a statement of facts that support the applicant's affirmation that the target is a foreign power or an agent of a foreign power.[9] The application must also set forth proposed "minimization" procedures, a detailed description of the nature of the information sought, and the types of communications to be monitored. The assistant to the president for national security affairs[10] must certify that the information sought is foreign intelligence information within the meaning of the act and is not obtainable by other means. Finally, the application must include the history, if any, of past applications for this same target, whether physical entry is necessary to accomplish the electronic surveillance, the types of surveillance devices to be used, the means by which they will be installed, and the period of time for which communications are to be monitored.

If the order sought is for surveillance of an "official" foreign power, and if the premises to be subject to the surveillance are owned, leased, or exclusively used by one of these targets, less information is required to obtain a court order.[11] Then there is no requirement that the application describe the nature of the communications sought, the type of communications to be monitored, the means by which the surveillance will be accomplished, or that it detail the types of surveillance devices to be employed.

In deciding whether to issue an order, the judge examines the application to determine whether there is probable cause to conclude that the target is a foreign power or an agent of a foreign power and that the facilities at which the surveillance is directed are or will be used by the target. If the target is a U.S. person, the judge must find that the certification by the assistant to the president for national security affairs is not "clearly erroneous."[12]

In most instances the judge's order approves electronic surveillance for ninety days, although a year is permitted if the target is an official foreign power. An extension may be granted on the same basis as the original order, except an extension for surveillance of nonofficial foreign powers may be for a year if probable cause is found to conclude that no communication of any U.S. person will be involved. The judge may assess compliance with the order at any time during the surveillance or at the end of the approved period.[13]

With a few exceptions, FISA has been generally praised as permitting effective intelligence gathering while providing sufficient Fourth Amendment protections for prospective targets of electronic surveillance.[14] It has been noted, however, that there are arguably two major gaps in coverage in the act: It does not explicitly regulate foreign intelligence physical searches; and it does not cover searches or surveillance engaged in by U.S. intelligence agencies abroad.[15]

Despite efforts to do so, FISA has not been amended to fill these gaps. Most important for present purposes, neither FISA nor any other U.S. legislation expressly regulates electronic surveillance abroad. Rather, constraints on electronic surveillance and other methods of intelligence gathering abroad have come from presidential executive orders (the latest of which was President Ronald Reagan's Executive Order 12333[16]), congressional oversight based on such legislation as the Intelligence Oversight Act of 1980,[17] and executive branch oversight through such mechanisms as the President's Foreign Intelligence Advisory Board[18] and the President's Intelligence Oversight Board.[19]

The debate between Congress and the executive branch over intelligence activities has centered primarily on two issues: (1) control over covert actions; and (2) the right of Congress to have access to sensitive intelligence information. With respect to the gathering of intelligence abroad, through electronic surveillance or other means, the executive branch has basically been given free rein. The legislative history of the National Intelligence Act of 1980, for example, reveals a congressional willingness to allow the president to approve physical searches of U.S. citizens abroad if "extraordinary circumstances require such collection to acquire foreign intelligence that is essential to the national security of the United States and that cannot reasonably be acquired by other means."[20]

If there are relatively few constraints on U.S. intelligence agencies with respect to the collection of intelligence, the situation is more problematical with respect to the availability and the dissemination of such information to government officials having primary responsibility for combatting terrorism. Similarly, there are concerns that such information, once collected and disseminated, may be subject to mandatory public disclosure. Specifically, provisions of the Privacy Act of 1974[21] raise questions about the dissemination of information regarding terrorist activities to foreign governments. These provisions do not clearly preclude such dissemination, but they do contain certain ambiguities that render applicable limits uncertain. Although these problems were identified over a decade ago,[22] they remain unresolved.

Foreign police officials have reportedly identified similar problems of dissemination of intelligence concerning international terrorism to officials in other countries arising under their national laws.[23] Complaints have also been raised that the Freedom of Information Act (FOIA)[24] contains ambiguities that call into question the authority of U.S. officials to protect from disclosure confidential information received by the U.S. government from foreign government agencies, especially those below the level of a national agency.[25] Foreign officials have often expressed strong views regarding the extent to which FOIA undermines efforts to gather intelligence and weakens confidence on the part of foreign officials in the intelligence-sharing process.[26] U.S. intelligence officials continue to express concern that FOIA poses a threat to the confidentiality of intelligence supplied by foreign intelligence sources, although there is agreement that the situation has improved.[27]

An operational issue that has arisen in the United States is whether a centralized data bank on terrorist activities should be created. Wayne Kerstetter has identified the problem:

> [T]his failure to routinely collate the information in the possession of federal agencies imposes inevitable limits on the U.S. capacity to realize the full benefits of the information gathered on terrorist activities and ultimately on the U.S. capacity to respond to the threat of terrorism. This failure also creates the danger of information being in the possession of several agencies which if brought together would be recognized as significant but when dispersed is not. It is unfortunate that having paid the economic and civil-liberties prices in collecting the information, we have not structured our affairs to provide the maximum benefits from the information collected. It is in fact a substantial disservice to ourselves and others.[28]

Resistance to creation of a centralized data bank on terrorism has come from civil liberties organizations that contend such a bank would unduly enhance the government's ability to intrude into the private lives of U.S. citizens. Kerstetter's response is that as data bases proliferate among a number of government agencies, proper data control becomes more difficult and thereby creates a greater threat to privacy rights. In his view, "the intelligence function is best controlled by careful attention to the articulation of sound operating guidelines and effective enforcement of the rules established," and this is best "facilitated by the centralization of intelligence data bases."[29]

A Conference on Legal Aspects of International Terrorism, sponsored by the Department of State and the Law Enforcement Assistance Administration with the American Society of International Law, and held on December 13–15, 1978, addressed this issue. At the end of the conference, the participants agreed on the following recommendation:

> The Executive Branch of the U.S. Government should consider developing a data base on terrorism by centralizing the collation and analyses of information about terrorists and terrorist activities currently collected by various U.S. agencies. Realistic guidelines should be developed defining what information is to be collected, analyzed, and disseminated to ensure that this activity is kept within appropriate limits. Care should be taken, in consultation with Congress, to ensure that appropriate legal authority has been established for this action and that effective guidelines for the activity are promulgated.[30]

To my knowledge, no action has been taken on this recommendation.

On the international level, different although related problems arise. For example, article 3 of the International Criminal Police Organization (Interpol) constitution provides that "[i]t is strictly forbidden for the organization to undertake any intervention or activities of a political, military, religious or racial character." Because of this restriction, Interpol in the past felt constrained to proceed cautiously in its involvement with law enforcement agencies combatting terrorism. Interpol would not participate in intelligence activity aimed at preventing terrorist acts; however, once a criminal act had occurred, it would assist in the efforts of law enforcement agencies to apprehend the responsible individuals. This policy also led Interpol to include in its files only those individuals who were directly implicated in a crime; individuals merely suspected of involvement in terrorist activity were excluded.[31]

This cautious approach greatly limited the scope of Interpol's files and the effectiveness of preventive action by the international police community. In addition, the "directly implicated" standard was imprecise—it was unclear whether it covered coconspirators, accessories, and sympathizers. In 1984, however, Interpol adopted a resolution that interpreted its constitution in such a way as to remove restrictions related to the political dimension of terrorism and to permit the organization to become more actively involved in combatting terrorism.[32] Interpol has now established a special section for terrorism.[33]

According to L. Paul Bremer III, U.S. ambassador-at-large for counterterrorism, these changes have had a beneficial effect. In 1985 Interpol began coordinating information on terrorism. The Federal Bureau of Investigation can now notify the Interpol secretariat of arrest warrants the United States has issued on terrorists, and Interpol then sends the names to all of its member countries.[34]

Interpol's activities to date, however, have focused exclusively on the actions and whereabouts of individual terrorists and on efforts to apprehend them. It has not collected data with a view to identifying states that support or sponsor terrorism; doing so arguably would contravene article 3 of its charter. There are, moreover, strong arguments to be made against involving Interpol in efforts to combat state-sponsored terrorism.[35] The organization would surely become embroiled in highly charged political controversies that would substantially reduce its effectiveness in carrying out its functions with respect to private acts of international terrorism, and states suspected of sponsorship would attempt to undermine its operations. Accordingly, with respect to the gathering, dissemination, and analysis of intelligence regarding state-sponsored terrorism, it may be preferable to consider alternatives to Interpol.

There has been considerable discussion over the appropriate arrangements for collaboration among intelligence officers.[36] Some have stressed the need for an international clearinghouse of information in order to permit law enforcement officials to track the whereabouts of terrorists. This central agency would stop short of being an international terrorist data bank, which, most experts agree, would not be feasible because of political factors. Government attitudes toward antiterrorist enforcement efforts are mercurial, varying with the political pressures of the moment, which leads most law enforcement officials to reject proposals for elaborate structure. Instead they tend to favor informal links between law enforcement officials as the best way to maintain the flexibility necessary to efficient activities.

There is evidence that these informal links have been developed and strengthened in recent years. Speaking at an American Bar Association (ABA) National Conference on Law in Relationship to Terrorism held in the summer of 1986,[37] William Webster, then director of the FBI, reported that at a 1985 meeting in The Hague between U.S. officials and ministers of the interior and justice from Western European countries, informal agreements were reached for greater sharing of intelligence. According to Webster, the U.S. effort at this meeting was to convince U.S. allies of the magnitude of the threat and to work toward a common analysis of it.[38]

Similarly, a positive step toward an international clearinghouse for intelligence information regarding terrorism was taken on April 24, 1986, when cabinet ministers from EEC countries agreed to step up their exchange of information on terrorism with the United States and other nonmember states.[39] A policy paper of the Atlantic Council has reported that "the U.S. Government is now able to transmit rapidly to foreign governments detailed information on the background and composition of terrorist groups, including 'mugshots' of individuals, to assist in the coordination of counterterrorist activities."[40] Most recently, Ambassador Bremer has gone so far as to state: "Among the interior ministers in Europe, within Interpol, within military organizations and intelligence agencies, the professionals are meeting each other and sharing tactics, intelligence, and ideas. There is, today, a counterterrorism network, and we are all benefitting from it."[41]

This network is starting to pay off: At the ABA conference, Webster reported that because of effective intelligence operations, the United States had been successful in 1985 in preventing six terrorist attacks against Americans abroad.[42] More recently, Ambassador Bremer reported that as of October 15, 1987, there had been a measurable drop in international terrorism over the previous eighteen months. He stated that terrorism in Western Europe during 1986 dropped "dramatically," over 33 percent.[43]

At the national level, too, the results are encouraging. According to Webster, for example, in 1976 and 1977 there were 100 terrorist attacks in the United States, and none was prevented. By contrast, 23 were prevented in 1985, and only seven succeeded.[44]

Nonetheless, the issue remains whether national law and policy as well as international arrangements currently strike the appropriate balance between how to provide law enforcement and security officials with sufficient authority and guidelines to discharge their responsibilities to combat terrorist activities on the one hand, and how to ensure the protection of such fundamental values as freedom of information and privacy on the other. The emergence of state-sponsored terrorism has made reconciling these competing interests a more urgent task than ever.

Notes

1. B. JENKINS, S.L. WILDHORN, & M. LAVIN, INTELLIGENCE CONSTRAINTS OF THE 1970s AND DOMESTIC TERRORISM (1982).

2. 50 U.S.C.A. §§ 1801–1811.

3. *Id.* § 1801(e)(1)(B).

4. *Id.* § 1801(a)(1)(A)(i). Although the act defines a foreign power to include groups engaged in international terrorism or activities in preparation therefor, *id.* § 1801(a)(4), surveillance without a warrant is limited to nations, factions, or entities recognized as being controlled by foreign governments. *Id.* § 1802(a)(1)(A)(ii).

5. *Id.* § 1802(a)(1)(B)(C).

6. *Id.* § 1805(e).

7. *Id.* § 1803(a).

8. *Id.* § 1803(b).

9. *See Id.* § 1801(a)(4), (5), and (6) and § 1804(a).

10. Or an executive branch official designated by the president from those officials dealing with national security or defense whose appointments were confirmed by the Senate. *Id.* § 1804(a)(7).

11. *Id.* § 1801(a)(1), (2), and (3) and 1804(b).

12. *Id.* § 1805(a)(5).

13. *Id.* § 1805(d)(1), (2), and (3).

14. *See, e.g.,* Shapiro, *The Foreign Intelligence Surveillance Act: Legislative Balancing of National Security and the Fourth Amendment,* 15 HARV. J. ON LEGIS. 119, 188–204 (1977); note, *Who's Listening: Proposals for Amending the Foreign Intelligence Surveillance Act,* 70 VIR. L. REV. 297 (1984).

15. Note, *Who's Listening: Proposals for Amending the Foreign Intelligence Surveillance Act, supra* note 14, at 330–35.

16. 3 C.F.R. 200 (1982).

17. 50 U.S.C. § 413.

18. Exec. Order No. 12,331, 3 C.F.R. 197 (1981).

19. Exec. Order No. 12,334, 3 C.F.R. 216 (1981).

20. S. 2284, 96th Cong., 2d Sess., 126 Cong. Rec. 2509–10 (daily ed. Feb. 8, 1980).

21. 5 U.S.C. § 552(a) *et seq.*

22. *See, e.g.,* Kerstetter, *Practical Problems of Law Enforcement,* Legal Aspects of International Terrorism 535, 541–43 (A. Evans & J. Murphy, eds. 1978); Kerstetter, *Terrorism and Intelligence,* Terrorism—an International Journal 109 (1979–80).

23. Kerstetter, *Practical Problems of Law Enforcement, supra* note 22, at 543–44.

24. 5 U.S.C. § 552(a) *et seq.*

25. Kerstetter, *Practical Problems of Law Enforcement, supra* note 22, at 543–44.

26. J. Murphy, Legal Aspects of International Terrorism: Summary Report of an International Conference 16 (1980).

27. J. Murphy, Summary Report of the American Bar Association Conference on Law in Relationship to Terrorism 26 (June 5, 6, and 7, 1986).

28. Kerstetter, *Terrorism and Intelligence, supra* note 22, at 111.

29. *Id.*

30. J. Murphy, *supra* note 26, at 19.

31. Kerstetter, *Practical Problems of Law Enforcement, supra* note 22, at 535.

32. Resolution on the Application of Article 3 of the Constitution adopted in September 1984 at the 53rd Interpol General Assembly Sessions.

33. *See* S. Bedlington, Combatting International Terrorism: U.S.-Allied Cooperation and Political Will 32 (Atlantic Council Policy Paper, 1986).

34. Bremer, *Counterterrorism: Strategy and Tactics,* 88 Dep't State Bull. 47, 49 (Jan. 1988).

35. Kerstetter, *Practical Problems of Law Enforcement, supra* note 22, at 538–39.

36. *See, e.g.,* J. Murphy, *supra* note 26, at 17–18.

37. J. Murphy, *supra* note 27, at 25.

38. *Id.*

39. N.Y. Times, Apr. 25, 1986, at A6, cols. 1–2.

40. S. Bedlington, *supra* note 33, at 31.

41. Bremer, *Counterterrorism: U.S. Policy and Proposed Legislation,* 88 Dep't State Bull 44 (Jan. 1988).

42. J. Murphy, *supra* note 27, at 25.

43. Bremer, *supra* note 41, at 44.

44. J. Murphy, *supra* note 27, at 24.

4

Quiet Diplomacy, Public Protest, and International and Transnational Claims

With this chapter we begin our consideration of possible responses to state-supported or state-sponsored terrorism. Here we explore the less coercive of possible responses: quiet diplomacy, public protest, and international and transnational claims. Later chapters turn to the more coercive responses: economic sanctions and military action.

Quiet Diplomacy and Public Protest

Quiet diplomacy is an important means of responding to international terrorism and has demonstrated its worth on a number of occasions. A substantial advantage of quiet diplomacy is that it avoids public confrontations, in which states are likely, for reasons of national pride, to adopt their most inflexible positions. It is undoubtedly the case that many of the most successful instances of quiet diplomacy have never become public knowledge—by definition, these efforts take place out of public view because their exposure may abort delicate negotiations toward resolution of a crisis. Nonetheless, there are a number of cases for which the results of such diplomacy and negotiations are now known, and they are impressive.

For example, in the wake of a series of hijacking incidents involving U.S. and Cuban airplanes and vessels during the late 1950s and early 1960s, the United States and Cuba entered into negotiations (by diplomatic notes through third parties) for their return. The particular focus was on an Electra airplane owned by Eastern Airlines that had been hijacked to Havana on July 24, 1961, and on a Cuban patrol vessel that had been hijacked to Key West.[1] Diplomatic correspondence between the two governments indicated a willingness on both sides to release the airplane and patrol boat. The Cuban government also expressed a desire to adopt "the most effective measures to avoid in the future the repetition of acts of piracy and seizure of ships and airplanes."[2]

The result of these negotiations was the 1973 United States–Cuba Memorandum of Understanding on Hijacking of Aircraft and Vessels and Other Offenses,[3] perhaps the most significant of several bilateral agreements specifically directed against the hijacking of aircraft or ships. The memorandum provides that any person who hijacks an aircraft or vessel registered under the law of one party to the territory of the other party shall either be returned to the party of registry or "be brought before the courts of the party whose territory he reached for trial in conformity with its laws for the offense punishable by the most severe penalty according to the circumstances and seriousness of the acts to which the Article refers." Thus, the memorandum incorporates the extradite-or-prosecute formula, but does so in a more meaningful way than do the multilateral antiterrorist conventions—unlike these, the U.S.-Cuba agreement requires that the accused actually be tried, not merely submitted "for the purpose of prosecution."

Under the memorandum, each party expressly recognizes an affirmative obligation to prevent the use of its territory as a base for committing the illegal acts specified.[4] Each party must bring to trial "with a view to severe punishment" any person who,

> within its territory, hereafter conspires to promote, or promotes, or prepares, or directs, or forms part of an expedition which from its territory or any other place carries out acts of violence or deprivation against aircraft or vessels of any kind or registration coming from or going to the territory of the other party or . . . carries out such acts or other similar unlawful acts in the territory of the other party.[5]

Finally, the memorandum severely limits the extent to which the hijacker's motivation may be taken into account by the country of arrival. The following may be given consideration:

any extenuating or mitigating circumstances in those cases in which the persons responsible for the acts were being sought for strictly political reasons and were in real and imminent danger of death without a viable alternative for leaving the country, provided there was no financial extortion or physical injury to the members of the crew, passengers, or other persons in connection with the hijacking.[6]

In 1976 the memorandum was denounced by Cuba on the ground that the United States had failed to control anti-Castro terrorists who had planted a bomb on a Cuban civilian aircraft.[7] Nonetheless, Cuba has continued to show in practice that hijackers still face imprisonment in Cuba or extradition to the United States.[8] To be sure, Cuba is still widely regarded as a state sponsor of terrorism, and no general rapprochement has taken place between the two countries. But the U.S.-Cuba memorandum stands as an example of the effectiveness of creative diplomacy in combatting terrorism.

The U.S.-Cuba agreement required use of intermediaries because the two countries do not have diplomatic relations. The go-between concept might be extended through demarches made to states enjoying close relations with states that sponsor terrorism to induce them to cease such sponsorship.

The most prominent of these potential intermediary states is the Soviet Union. There are encouraging signs that the USSR is re-thinking its position on international terrorism. For example, the Soviet Union joined with the United States and Third World countries to defeat a Syrian proposal designed to confer legitimacy on international terrorism if undertaken in the cause of "national liberation."[9] Soviet opposition was a major factor in inducing Syria to revise its draft resolution to eliminate the offensive passages.

Soviet representatives have also reportedly expressed a willingness to distinguish between ideology and acts of terrorism and to accept the principle that some means are unacceptable no matter how just the cause.[10] Among the methods apparently deserving of absolute Soviet censure were the bombing of innocent people, the abuse of diplomatic privileges, and the use of biological and chemical or nuclear weapons.[11] More specifically, according to Ambassador Bremer,[12] the Soviet Union has condemned some recent acts of terrorism, including a takeover of a Pan American flight in Karachi, Pakistan, and a grenade attack in 1986 against Israeli soldiers near the Western

Wall in Jerusalem. Ambassador Bremer also reports that the Soviet Union played a helpful role in drafting new antiterrorist conventions on maritime and airport safety. In a recent speech, Mikhail Gorbachev went so far as to propose the creation of a United Nations tribunal to investigate acts of international terrorism.[13]

Other states might play a useful role as intermediaries between states sponsoring terrorism and their potential targets. Algeria, it will be remembered, did this in helping to bring Iran's detention of U.S. diplomats as hostages to an end.[14] Other Islamic states might be able to serve as intermediaries, especially with respect to such state sponsors of terrorism as Iran, Libya, and Syria. Moreover, an effort should be made to regularize the use of intermediaries, rather than to turn to them on an ad hoc, reactive basis. Demarches by state intermediaries are likely to be most effective if made when a state is contemplating sponsoring terrorism but has not yet made a decision to do so.

Quiet diplomacy might also be useful to encourage states to fulfill their international obligations with respect to combatting terrorism. For example, France and Italy have reportedly made secret deals with terrorists and their sponsors in an effort to spare their French and Italian citizens from attack in exchange for giving terrorists freedom of movement and freedom from arrest.[15] Such bargaining should be protested vehemently—at first quietly and then, if necessary, publicly. (Also, as discussed in the next section, such deals might be the basis for an international claim against the states entering into them.) Public protest would occur if quiet diplomacy failed and the state approached nevertheless engaged in the sponsorship of terrorism. The effort here would be similar to the "mobilization of shame" technique applied to egregious violators of human rights. Ideally it would be multilateral rather than unilateral.

International Claims

There is no doubt that state-sponsored terrorism violates international law. The General Assembly's Declaration on Principles of International Law Concerning Friendly Relations and Co-operation Among States in Accordance with the Charter of the United Nations—generally regarded as an authoritative interpretation of broad principles of international law expressed in the UN Charter—provides in pertinent part:

> Every State has the duty to refrain from organizing, instigating, assisting or participating in acts of civil strife or terrorist acts in another State or acquiescing in organized activities within its present territory directed towards the commission of such acts, when the acts referred to in the present paragraph involve a threat or use of force.[16]

The recent General Assembly and Security Council resolutions unanimously condemning terrorism also highlight the illegality of state sponsorship. Similarly, the findings of scholarly studies demonstrate state responsibility for sponsoring or supporting terrorism.[17]

Therefore, given that state-sponsored terrorism is clearly illegal, protests set forth in diplomatic correspondence or raised in international organizations should fully state the facts and the applicable international law, explain why the accused state is in violation, and challenge the state to refute the charge. Because of the problematic nature of adjudicatory remedies in this area, protests in diplomatic correspondence and in international organizations may be the most effective means of bringing claims based on traditional state responsibility principles. Most protests against terrorist acts, however, contain neither a full exposition of the facts nor of the law that has been violated. This is unfortunate, because a strong case that peremptory norms of international law have been violated lends substantial weight to a diplomatic protest. Moreover, a well-documented legal case against a state sponsoring terrorism, presented initially through diplomatic channels, may lay the foundation for other responses should the state responsible fail to desist.[18]

Adjudication of international claims in arbitral or judicial tribunals presents obstacles, but should not be ruled out completely. State responsibility for injuries caused by terrorist attack has been the subject of arbitrations in the past,[19] and it is not inconceivable that it could be again. At the least, the procedural flexibility, control by the parties of the proceedings and the law applied, and other inherent advantages of international arbitration over court proceedings might induce states to submit some of the issues between them to arbitration and lessen the incentive to turn to terrorism.[20] Possible recourse to the International Court of Justice (ICJ) is complicated by the heated debate over its decision in *Nicaragua v. United States* and by the U.S. withdrawal from the court's compulsory jurisdiction.[21] It should be remembered, however, that the ICJ played a useful role in the Iran hostage crisis. Moreover, there are clauses in several of the antiterrorist conventions that give the court jurisdiction to consider disputes over their interpretation or application.[22] Indeed, as of January 1, 1989, Iran was still a party to the Convention on the Prevention of Crimes Against Internationally Protected Persons, Including Diplomatic Agents,[23] whose compromissory clause was one basis cited by the United States for the court's jurisdiction in the *U.S. v. Iran* case.[24] In addition, a similar clause in the U.S.-Iran Treaty of Amity, Economic Relations, and Consular Rights[25] was specifically cited by the ICJ as a basis for its jurisdiction.

Consideration should also be given to the possibilities of suit— either before an arbitral tribunal or an international court—against states that, by their failure to fulfill their international obligations, merely support rather than sponsor terrorism. For example, a good argument could be made that during the course of the *Achille Lauro* incident, Egypt, Italy, and Yugoslavia avoided their responsibilities to the United States and to the world community. Perhaps these countries should have been subject to suit for these violations. To be sure, some observers have charged that the United States, in intercepting the airliner carrying the hijackers of the *Achille Lauro* to safety, violated international law[26] (a charge examined later). Accordingly, in any suit brought against any of these states by the United States, this charge might be subject to adjudication.

Claims might also be brought before regional tribunals, such as the European Court of Human Rights or the European Court of Justice. Some of the special deals allegedly made by France and Italy with terrorists (they reportedly were permitted to use France and Italy as staging grounds for attacks provided they did not strike at French or Italian targets[27]) may constitute violations of the European Convention on Human Rights or the Treaty Establishing the European Economic Community (the Rome Treaty). These arrangements arguably violated both the letter and the spirit of the convention and the treaty.[28] The United States is not a party to either of these instruments, but some of its close allies—the very states most affected by the deals—are and would therefore have standing to pursue such claims.

Transnational Litigation

The possibility of civil remedies in national courts against terrorists and the states sponsoring them is a subject just beginning to receive systematic attention. Among the many issues arising in this area are these: Who might be the targets of civil remedies—countries, groups, or individuals? Would it be possible to have a common law remedy (not based on statute)? Under what circumstances can individuals be said to violate international law? Does international law provide for a private right of action? If there is a private right of action, is it limited to compensatory damages, or are punitive damages and injunctive relief available?[29]

With respect to the possibility of private litigation in the United States as a response to terrorism, the limited precedent available is mixed. The legislation in this area is the Judiciary Act of 1789 (ch. 20 9(b), 1 stat. 73, 77 (1789), *codified* at 28 U.S.C. § 1350). Under this Alien Tort Statute, as it is commonly called, Congress provided: "The district courts shall have original jurisdiction of any civil action by an alien for a tort only, committed in violation of the law of nations or a treaty of the United States." The statute requires the presence of three factors for a suit to lie: an alien plaintiff, a tort, and a violation of the law of nations. The issue, then, would seem to be whether terrorism is a violation of international law—in other words, is there an internationally protected right of an individual to be free from terrorism?

This issue arose in *Tel-Oren v. Libya*.[30] There, the survivors and representatives of persons murdered in an armed attack on a civilian bus in Israel brought suit against Libya, the Palestine Liberation Organization (PLO), and three Arab-American organizations for alleged multiple acts of terrorism, which the plaintiffs asserted were a violation of the law of nations. The district court dismissed on numerous grounds, including lack of subject matter jurisdiction, reasoning that for the suit to lie, international law would itself have to provide a private remedy, which it did not. The District of Columbia Circuit Court of Appeals affirmed the district court *per curiam*, but Judges Robert Bork, Harry Edwards, and Roger Robb wrote three concurring opinions that differed sharply in their rationales. Judge Bork agreed with the district court that a private right of action had to be found in the governing norm of international law in order for a plaintiff to have access to domestic courts. Judge Robb was of the opinion that the political-question doctrine barred the court from assuming jurisdiction because the issue of appropriate remedies against Libya, the PLO, and the three organizations was properly to be decided by the executive branch.

Although Judge Edwards disagreed with the reasoning of both Judge Bork and Judge Robb, he nonetheless joined in the court's decision, on several grounds. Judge Edwards found that the PLO was not a recognized state and that it did not act under color of any recognized state's law. Therefore it had no legal personality under international law, and even if there were an international norm against terrorism, it would not bind the PLO. Judge Edwards also believed that individual responsibility would lie under international law only if the person was acting under color of state law, even if in violation of it. Finally, he also found that under current law, terrorist attacks did not amount to a law-of-nations violation. (In footnotes, both Judge Bork and Judge Edwards summarily dismissed the cause of action against Libya on the ground that it was barred by the Foreign Sovereign Immunities Act.[31])

The various opinions in the *Tel-Oren* case suggest that the only clear possible defendant in a terrorism case under § 1350 would be an individual who committed a terrorist act under the color of state law. Even then, no cause of action would lie if the court agreed with Judge Edwards' conclusion that terrorist attacks do not currently violate the law of nations.

But is Judge Edwards mistaken? Plaintiffs in *Tel-Oren* alleged that the terrorists took passengers of a bus hostage, tortured them, and murdered them. As earlier chapters have shown, the world community is fast reaching a consensus that terrorism, especially in the form of hostage taking, is impermissible under any circumstances.[32] The United Nations General Assembly's rejection of the Syrian initiative, discussed earlier, is the latest evidence of this developing consensus.

An even stronger consensus has developed with respect to the proposition that torture is a violation of international law. The Second Circuit confirmed this trend in the landmark case of *Filartiga v. Pena-Irala*,[33] in an opinion whose analysis of § 1350 was accepted by Judge Edwards but rejected by Judge Bork in *Tel-Oren*. In *Filartiga* the court held that plaintiff, a citizen of Paraguay, had a cause of action against defendant, another citizen of Paraguay, for wrongful death. The court found that "deliberate torture perpetrated under color of official authority violates universally accepted norms of the international law of human rights, regardless of the nationality of the parties."[34] Upon remand the district court awarded the plaintiff substantial compensatory and punitive damages.

Moreover, judicial authority since *Tel-Oren* has rejected Judge Bork's contention that for a cause of action to lie under § 1350, international law must provide for a private remedy.[35] Commentators have pointed out that there is no international consensus on remedies even with respect to torture, so that if Judge Bork is right, *Filartiga* was wrongly decided. But recent decisions support *Filartiga*'s reasoning rather than that of Judge Bork.[36]

Litigation was pending in 1989 in a court in New York that may further clarify the possibility of private suits against private organizations. In *Klinghoffer v. Palestine Liberation Organization*,[37] the court has been asked to rule on whether it has jurisdiction over a suit for damages for the murder of Leon Klinghoffer by Palestinian terrorists aboard the *Achille Lauro*. The action was brought by the Klinghoffer family against the PLO.

The problems raised by the opinions in the *Tel-Oren* case are formidable enough, but Professor Harold Koh in a provocative article[38] has pointed out others, noting that the legal obstacles to obtaining a civil remedy against terrorism through the judiciary constitute a veritable "minefield" for those seeking compensatory and punitive damages.[39] Professor Koh also has suggested that Congress, rather than the courts, is the appropriate institution to resolve these problems—Congress has the resources to gather facts and consider all points of view through hearings, at which human rights activists and U.S. and foreign officials could testify. As models or general guidelines for a statute providing comprehensive civil and criminal remedies against terrorism, Professor Koh has pointed to the Racketeer Influenced and Corrupt Organizations Act (RICO), civil rights laws, antitrust statutes, and the Foreign Sovereign Immunities Act.

Particular attention has been focused on the possibility of utilizing the civil remedies provisions of RICO[40] against groups supporting terrorists. These provisions authorize government suits and private treble-damage actions by persons injured in their business or property against RICO "enterprises" engaging in a "pattern of racketeering,"[41] which is defined to include "any act or threat involving murder, kidnapping . . . arson . . . or extortion."[42] An "enterprise" includes "any . . . group of individuals associated in fact although not a legal entity."[43] The U.S. government has successfully used the criminal action provisions of RICO against terrorist organizations[44] and is reportedly contemplating invoking the civil remedies provisions to seek injunctions limiting the activities and obtaining the forfeiture of assets of other organizations supporting terrorist groups.[45] Whether this approach would be successful is unclear. Accordingly, the possibility of either amending RICO to expressly cover organizations supporting terrorists or of enacting separate legislation—such as a terrorist organizational liability statute—is under active consideration.[46]

The use of civil remedies against terrorists and states supporting terrorists is a new concept that requires a great deal more study. As Professor Koh's article admirably demonstrates, the issues are manifold and complex. One overarching issue is whether enacting comprehensive legislation providing for civil remedies against terrorist organizations and states sponsoring terrorism might set a precedent that could redound to the detriment of U.S. citizens and the U.S. government. Other countries might in response promulgate legislation along similar lines, but their definitions of terrorism would reflect ideological predilections and thus might differ significantly from definitions in U.S. legislation or governmental pronouncements.

Notes

1. The factual background of this case is summarized in Cardozo, *Judicial Deference to State Department Suggestions: Recognition of Prerogative or Abdication to Usurper?* 48 CORNELL L.Q. 461, 464–67 (1963).

2. For copies of this correspondence, *see* 45 DEP'T STATE BULL. 407, 408 (1961).

3. 24 U.S.T. 737, T.I.A.S. No. 7579.

4. *Id.* art. 2.

5. *Id.*

6. *Id.* art. 4.

7. *See* editorial, Washington Post, October 19, 1976, at A18, col. 1.

8. *See, e.g.,* N.Y. Times, Sept. 18, 1980, at A20, col. 1.

9. *See* N.Y. Times, Dec. 2, 1987, at A17, col. 1.

10. S. Bedlington, Combatting International Terrorism: U.S.-Allied Cooperation and Political Will 57–58 (Atlantic Council Nov. 1986).

11. *Id.*

12. Bremer, *Counterterrorism: Strategy and Tactics,* 88 Dep't State Bull. 47, 49 (Jan. 1988).

13. N.Y. Times, Oct. 8, 1987, at A1, col. 5.

14. *See* Cutler, *Negotiating the Iranian Settlement,* 67 A.B.A.J. 996, 998 (Aug. 1981).

15. S. Bedlington, *supra* note 10, at 36.

16. G.A. Res. 2625, 25 U.N. GAOR Supp. (No. 28) 121, U.N. Doc. A/ 8028 (1970).

17. The definitive article on this subject is Lillich and Paxman, *State Responsibility for Injuries to Aliens Occasioned by Terrorist Activities,* 26 Am. U.L. Rev. 217 (1977).

18. Some of these points were suggested to me by Richard Lillich, Howard W. Smith Professor of Law, University of Virginia, through correspondence.

19. See Lillich and Paxman, *supra* note 17.

20. For a quite extraordinary example of the possibilities in this regard, *see* the United Nations secretary-general's ruling in the *Rainbow Warrior Affair* between France and New Zealand, 26 I.L.M. 1346 (Sept. 1987).

21. Military and Paramilitary Activities in and Against Nicaragua (Nicar. v. U.S.), Merits, 1986 I.C.J. Rep. 14 (Judgment of June 27).

22. *See, e.g.,* article 12 of the Convention for Suppression of Unlawful Seizure of Aircraft, Dec. 16, 1970, 22 U.S.T. 1641, T.I.A.S. No. 7192, 860 U.N.T.S. 105; article 16, International Convention Against the Taking of Hostages, Dec. 17, 1979, ___ U.S.T. ___, T.I.A.S. No. ___, ___ U.N.T.S. ___.

23. Dec. 14, 1973, 28 U.S.T. 1975, T.I.A.S. No. 8532, 1035 U.N.T.S. 167.

24. United States Diplomatic and Consular Staff in Teheran (U.S. v. Iran), 1980 I.C.J. Rep. 3.

25. Article XXI, para. 2, 8 U.S.T. 899, 909 T.I.A.S. No. 3853. The court did not decide whether article 13 of the Convention on Protected Persons provided a basis for exercise of its jurisdiction. I.C.J. judgment, *supra* note 24, at 28.

26. *See, e.g.,* Schachter, *In Defense of International Rules on the Use of Force,* 53 U. Chi. L. Rev. 113, 140 (1986).

27. S. Bedlington, *supra* note 10, at 36.

28. For example, the European Convention on Human Rights and Fundamental Freedoms, Nov. 4, 1950, Europ. T.S. No. 5, reaffirms in its preamble the parties' "profound belief in those Fundamental Freedoms

which are the foundation of justice and peace in the world" and in article 2 proclaims that "[e]veryone's right to life shall be protected by law." Special deals with terrorists are hardly consistent with these provisions. Also, the professed goal of terrorists to disrupt the economies of their target states is incompatible with the goal of the European Economic Community, proclaimed in article 2 of the Treaty Establishing the European Economic Community, March 25, 1957, Office for Official Publications of the European Community, Treaties Establishing the European Communities (1979), as amended by the Treaty (signed on June 12, 1985) Concerning the Accession of Spain and Portugal, "to promote throughout the Community a harmonious development of economic activities, a continuous and balanced expansion, an increase in stability, an accelerated raising of the standard of living and closer relations between the States belonging to it."

29. These questions were raised by Theodore Olson, moderator for the panel on civil remedies against terrorists and actions supporting terrorists at the American Bar Association's National Conference on Law in Relationship to Terrorism. *See* J. MURPHY, SUMMARY REPORT OF THE AMERICAN BAR ASSOCIATION NATIONAL CONFERENCE ON LAW IN RELATIONSHIP TO TERRORISM 15 (June 5, 6, and 7, 1986).

30. 726 F.2d 774 (D.C. Cir. 1984).

31. For Judge Edwards' footnote, *see id.* at 775–76; for Judge Bork's footnote, *see id.* at 805.

32. This is especially demonstrated by S.C. Res. 579, 40 U.N. SCOR (2637th mtg.) at 24–25, U.N. Doc. S/17, 685 (1985). By this resolution the Security Council condemned *"unequivocally* all acts of hostage-taking and abduction"; called for the immediate safe release of all hostages; affirmed the obligation of states in whose territory hostages are taken to take steps to secure their safe release and to prevent such actions in the future; appealed to all states that had not yet done so to become parties to the antiterrorist conventions; and urged further international cooperation in order "to facilitate the prevention, prosecution, and punishment of all acts of hostage-taking and abduction as manifestations of international terrorism."

33. 636 F.2d 876 (2d Cir. 1980).

34. *Id.* at 878.

35. *See, e.g.,* Forti v. Suarez-Mason, 672 F. Supp. 1531 (N.D. Cal. 1987).

36. *Id.* and Rappaport v. Suarez-Mason, C-87-2266 JPU (N.D. Cal. Sept. 9, 1987).

37. 27801/85 (N.Y. Sup. Ct.). I am informed by the clerk of the New York Supreme Court (a trial court in the New York court system) that the Klinghoffer suit against the PLO is currently "on hold," pending further developments in Klinghoffer v. S.N.C. Achille Lauro, 85 Civ. 9303 (S.D.N.Y.), a negligence action against the S.N.C. Achille Lauro shipping line. For an

earlier discussion of the two suits, *see* Stille, *The PLO: A Suit Provides an Inside Look*, National Law Journal, Dec. 28, 1987–Jan. 4, 1988, at 1.

38. Koh, *Civil Remedies for Uncivil Wrongs: Combatting Terrorism Through Transnational Public Law Litigation*, 22 TEX. INT'L. L.J. 169 (1987).

39. *Id.* at 181–85.

40. 18 U.S.C. §§ 1961–1968 (1984).

41. *Id.* § 1964(c) (1982).

42. *Id.* § 1961(1), (5).

43. *Id.* § 1961(4).

44. U.S. v. Bagaric, 706 F.2d 42 (2d Cir. 1983) (Serbo-Croatian terrorists extorting contributions from U.S. residents).

45. *See* J. MURPHY, *supra* note 29, at 17.

46. An American Bar Association working group on terrorism, chaired by Harris Weinstein, Esq., of Covington & Burling, Washington, D.C., is actively considering this along with several other possibilities.

5

Economic Sanctions

This chapter deals with the more forceful responses to international terrorism. Economic sanctions are often viewed as the peaceful—if forceful—alternative to the use of armed force, and the United States is unquestionably in the vanguard with respect to their use for political ends. Economic sanctions have been imposed against the Soviet Union and to protest apartheid and other egregious violations of human rights.[1]

Since the 1970s, moreover, economic sanctions have been a prominent part of the U.S. response to foreign involvement in international terrorism. Numerous congressional statutes authorize or require the executive branch to limit various economic relationships with countries the Secretary of State has determined to be supporters of terrorism.[2] This group today includes Libya, North Korea, Syria, South Yemen, Iran, and Cuba.

Some commentators have been sharply critical of the effectiveness of economic sanctions.[3] Others, especially recently, have had kinder words to say for them.[4] We shall return to this issue later in the chapter.

Uses Against States Sponsoring
International Terrorism

Perhaps the most noteworthy use of economic sanctions by the United States against a state sponsoring international terrorism was the U.S. response to Iran in 1979 when it seized the U.S. embassy in Teheran and took personnel hostage.[5] More recently, the United States has intensified such responses. President Reagan's national emergency declaration of January 1986[6] prohibited virtually all economic transactions with Libya and froze Libyan assets subject to U.S. jurisdiction. Similarly, the United States tightened controls on exports to Iran in 1984[7] and strengthened sanctions against Syria in November 1986 and June 1987,[8] although none of these measures was as sweeping as those imposed against Libya. On the whole, the United States has applied these sanctions unilaterally. Some Western European states have taken action against Libya and Syria, but these efforts have been modest.

The major multilateral step toward sanctioning supporters of terrorism has been taken with respect to the hijacking of civilian aircraft. Early efforts to conclude a convention that would provide for the imposition of sanctions against states that failed to extradite a hijacker found within their territory or to submit the case to their competent authorities for the purpose of prosecution were unsuccessful. On July 17, 1978, however, the heads of state and government participating in the Bonn Economic Summit (Canada, France, the Federal Republic of Germany, Italy, Japan, the United Kingdom, and the United States [the Summit Countries]) agreed upon a declaration that has come to be known as the Bonn Declaration on Hijacking. The declaration provides:

> The Heads of State and Government, concerned about terrorism and the taking of hostages, declare that their governments will intensify their joint efforts to combat international terrorism. To this end, in cases where a country refuses extradition or prosecution of those who have hijacked an aircraft and/or does not return such aircraft, the Heads of State and Government are jointly resolved that their governments shall take immediate action to cease all flights to that country. At the same time, their governments will initiate action to halt all in-coming flights from that country, or from any country of the airlines of the country concerned. They urge other governments to join them in the commitment.[9]

Although there is some disagreement on this point, most commentators agree that the Bonn Declaration is not a binding legal instrument, but rather a statement of policy that expresses the intent of the Summit Countries to take action when, subsequent to a hijacking, other states have failed to live up to their obligations under it. Follow-up efforts have succeeded in obtaining widespread support for the declaration and in inducing additional countries to become parties to the ICAO conventions.

The first test of the Bonn Declaration came on July 20, 1981, when the heads of state and government meeting at the Ottawa Economic Summit considered the March 1981 hijacking of a Pakistan International Airlines aircraft to Afghanistan. Recalling and reaffirming the principles set forth in the 1978 Bonn Declaration, they stated that the action of the Afghan regime, both during the incident and subsequently (in giving refuge to the hijackers), "was and is a flagrant breach of its international obligations under the Hague Convention to which Afghanistan is a party and constitutes a serious threat to air safety."[10] Accordingly, the proposal was made to "suspend all flights to and from Afghanistan in implementation of the Bonn Declaration unless Afghanistan immediately takes steps to comply with its obligations"[11] and a call issued to "all states which share their concern for air safety to take appropriate action to persuade Afghanistan to honor its obligations."[12] The United States favored an immediate application of the Bonn Declaration sanctions. However, France, the Federal Republic of Germany, and the United Kingdom—the only countries among the seven to whose territories Ariana Afghan Airlines flew—maintained they could not employ sanctions without violating the terms of their bilateral air transit agreements with Afghanistan. These states instead gave Afghanistan a year's notice of their intent to terminate the air transit agreements.[13] On November 30, 1982, all three implemented the Bonn Declaration by suspending all air traffic with Afghanistan.[14]

Prior to imposition of the sanctions, Pakistan announced it had apprehended one of the three hijackers near the Pakistan-Afghanistan border.[15] After sanctions were applied, Ariana, the Afghan national airline, approached several other Western European countries in an attempt to obtain alternative traffic rights, but no countries granted such rights, and Ariana flights to Western Europe ceased entirely. In mid-1984 Kabul Radio announced that one of the three hijackers had been executed in Kabul on a conviction of murder unrelated to the hijacking. Though there is some question as to truth of this assertion, if true, it left only one of the three hijackers alive and at large at that time. The sanctions remained in effect until 1986, when they were quietly terminated.

An incident in which application of the Bonn Declaration was threatened—with significant effect—has received little attention. On November 25, 1981, approximately 50 armed mercenaries raided the airport near Victoria, the capital of the Seychelles, in an apparent coup attempt. The raid was unsuccessful, and in order to escape the mercenaries commandeered an Air India jetliner that had landed at the airport during the fighting and ordered it to fly to South Africa. Upon arrival of the plane in Durban, the passengers and crew were released unharmed. The 44 mercenaries who had taken over the plane were taken into custody, but a few days later 39 were released without charge. The other 5 were charged with kidnapping and released on bail. There were no charges filed relating to the hijacking itself.

The United States government strongly protested, requested "prompt and severe punishment" for the hijackers, and pointed out South Africa's obligations under the Hague Convention. The next day a State Department spokesman announced that the U.S. government was consulting with the Summit Countries as to possible application of the Bonn Declaration. Reportedly, the British and U.S. governments warned South Africa privately that if it did not prosecute or extradite the hijackers, it might be subject to Bonn Declaration sanctions. Apparently in response to this pressure, South Africa announced on December 6 that the 44 mercenaries could still be charged with hijacking, which indeed was done by January 1982. Trials were held in the spring of 1982, and 42 of the defendants were found guilty and sentenced to prison terms ranging from five to thirty years.

Since the Afghanistan and South African cases, the Bonn Declaration has been abandoned as a sanctions device. In February 1987 the U.S. Federal Aviation Agency compiled a partial list that included 17 outstanding hijacking cases involving 9 countries in which the status of the hijackers was unknown or in which the hijackers had been granted asylum. Yet the Bonn Declaration was not invoked as to any of them.

Perhaps the case that best demonstrates some of the difficulties arose when the Bonn Declaration was not applied to Lebanon for its failure to apprehend and extradite or prosecute the hijackers of TWA flight 847. The hijacking began on June 14, 1985, when two Lebanese Shiites hijacked the plane shortly after takeoff from Athens en route to Rome. Over the next three days, the hijackers—their number increased by Shiite militiamen who boarded the plane in Beirut—ordered the plane flown back and forth between Algiers and Beirut on two successive round trips. During this time they released all but 40 of the 153 hostages on board and, during the second trip to Beirut, murdered U.S. Navy diver Robert Stethem. When the plane finally came to rest at Beirut on June 17, the remaining 39 hostages, all U.S. nationals, were removed to various locations in Beirut under guard of Shiite militiamen.

Geoffrey Levitt has summarized the difficulties that then arose:

> As the nominal government of Lebanon went through the motions of addressing the crisis while the real players went about their business in almost total disregard of Lebanese government actions, the implications of the situation began to emerge more fully. In the chaotic state of Lebanese politics, the local "authorities"—those political and security forces with an ability to control and influence the situation at the site of the hijacking—were operating on the basis of a completely different set of assumptions from the typical government faced with such a problem. To these authorities, the hijacking was not a criminal/security problem to be resolved as quickly as possible through the neutralization and/or apprehension of the hijackers and the safe release of the hostages. Rather, it was above all a political opportunity to be exploited through alliance with the hijackers and partial adoption of their demands, while presenting to the rest of the world the picture of honest brokers and mediators trying to consider the interests of all "sides." Further complications arose from the fact that the chief demand of those in control of the TWA hostages was directed not against the U.S. government, whose nationals and flag aircraft had been seized, but against a third party, Israel.[16]

Despite these many difficulties, a resolution of the crisis was eventually reached: The hostages were released through Damascus, Israel released a number of Palestinian detainees in stages, and the United States stated that it "reaffirms its longstanding support for the preservation of Lebanon, its Government, its stability, and its security, and for the mitigation of the suffering of its people."[17]

Even before resolution of the crisis, the hijackers of TWA 847 had disappeared into West Beirut, and the issue of how they might be apprehended and prosecuted became acute after release of the hostages. Again Levitt has pinpointed the problem:

> But some very troubling questions were left in the wake of the release of the U.S. hostages. How could normal follow-up processes of apprehending and prosecuting perpetrators be undertaken when the authorities formally responsible for such steps did not even have the capacity to conduct a routine criminal trial? How could these processes be set into motion when the original hijackers, still even before the conclusion of the incident, had merged into a veritable crowd of accomplices and vanished into the *terra incognita* of West Beirut, where the government's authority ran very shallow indeed? Perhaps most unsettling of all, how could normal law enforcement measures against the hijackers even be contemplated when the man chiefly responsible for such measures, Lebanese Minister of Justice Nabih Berri, was himself arguably an accomplice to the hijacking? (As Secretary of State Shultz said at a press conference the evening the hostages were released, "I think we have some sorting out to do about Mr. Berri.") Given these realities, what could justify, and what would be the point of, imposing sanctions against a government that clearly had practically no control over the situation in the first place? In short, how could all of the standard international anti-hijacking mechanisms embodied in instruments like the Hague Convention and the Bonn Declaration be applied to the TWA 847 case?[18]

On July 1, the day after the hostages were released, the United States announced that Lebanese airlines would no longer be permitted to fly to the United States and that no flights by any airline would be permitted between the United States and Lebanon. The United States also undertook numerous diplomatic demarches to secure support for this embargo of the Beirut airport. As Levitt has noted, however, the initial rationale for the U.S. action was that purely from a security point of view, the Beirut airport increased the terrorist threat to all civil aviation in Europe and the Middle East— hence it should be subject to a quarantine. But the measures applied by the United States were substantially the same as those called for by the Bonn Declaration when a country refuses to extradite or prosecute hijackers.

Later statements by U.S. officials, moreover, seemed to base application of the measures on Lebanon's failure to apprehend and prosecute the hijackers, despite the U.S. demand made almost immediately following release of the hostages that the Lebanese authorities bring the hijackers to justice. The difficulty with this rationale was that Lebanon's failure to act was due more to its incapacity to do so than to an actual refusal on the part of responsible authorities. This factor, along with a variety of others, resulted in no other government joining in the boycott of the Beirut airport.

Although most commentators agree that the Bonn Declaration is not a binding legal instrument, it is noteworthy that the document is mandatory in tone and contains no express provision allowing a Summit Country discretion in deciding whether to apply sanctions against a country that "refuses extradition or prosecution." To be sure, Lebanon never officially refused to prosecute (a request for extradition was never made), and therefore arguably the terms of the declaration had not been met. There is no evidence, however, that legal considerations played any role in the refusal of the Summit Countries to join the U.S. boycott. The factor that apparently was decisive has been identified by Levitt:

> The policies of Western governments taken as a whole in the aftermath of the TWA 847 hijacking revealed some fundamental weaknesses in international counterterrorism cooperation. Despite the successful U.S. handling of the hijacking and hostage crisis itself, with the support of the allies, the Western response following the resolution of the incident was weak and divided. The U.S. Government exacerbated the inherent political difficulties of the situation by failing to present coherently and convincingly the mixed motivations—civil aviation security on the one hand, law enforcement and antihijacking policy on the other—underlying its campaign to boycott the airport.
>
> Clearly the actions of the Lebanese government simply did not and could not fit the Bonn Declaration paradigm of a government willfully abetting and harboring hijackers; rather its actions represented feeble efforts to make the best of a situation in which that government was in reality merely one player—and far from the strongest—contending for supremacy in a war-torn, fragmented society. The law enforcement and antihijacking aspect of the U.S. quarantine thus appeared inappropriate and bullying—an image skillfully played upon by Lebanese and Arab diplomacy. The moral wind was thereby taken out of the sails of any possible invocation of the Bonn Declaration against Lebanon. Conversely, the intense political manner in which the United

States pursued its international campaign against Beirut Airport, coupled with the campaign's undertone of punitive sanctions against a recalcitrant Lebanon, undermined any effect the United States might have derived from presenting the campaign as motivated by disinterested security concerns.[19]

What, then, can be made of the experience under the Bonn Declaration? Clearly, it has not been a resounding success. But the quick conclusion that it has been an utter failure is unwarranted. The sanctions applied against Afghanistan did have some effect, albeit not as much as idealists might have wished. The threatened application of Bonn Declaration sanctions against South Africa, by contrast, apparently had the full desired effect. Reliance on the instrument as a possible justification of sanctions against Lebanon, the record indicates, was simply misplaced.

Further, the Bonn Declaration is directed against state *support* rather than state *sponsorship* of terrorism. As we have seen, the moral case for applying the document against Lebanon was weak and contributed in no small measure to the unwillingness of other Summit Countries to join the United States. The strength of the moral case for levying economic sanctions against a state sponsoring terrorism, however, is great—which means the time has perhaps come to reconsider the possibility of arrangements that would *mandate* the imposition of economic sanctions against states sponsoring terrorism. As discussed earlier, a substantial but ultimately unsuccessful effort to mandate such sanctions as a matter of U.S. domestic law was made in 1978 through S. 2236, An Act to Combat International Terrorism.[20] More recently, Senator Frank Lautenberg introduced a bill[21] that would have required the executive branch to impose economic sanctions against states supporting terrorism. The administration opposed this legislation,[22] and it appears unlikely to be enacted into law.

Such legislation raises complex issues of constitutional separation of powers and of the appropriate amount of discretion the executive branch should have in this area, issues that are beyond the scope of this book. What is addressed here is the desirability of establishing a *multilateral* arrangement that would mandate the imposition of economic sanctions under certain circumstances.

The history of efforts to this end is not encouraging: Proposals to conclude an independent sanctions convention for the ICAO conventions advanced in 1973 at the Rome Security Conference and at the ICAO Extraordinary Assembly were unsuccessful. Other comparable proposals have met a similar fate.[23] It is not surprising, however, that efforts in a United Nations specialized agency would prove fruitless, especially in the political atmosphere that prevailed during the 1970s. Even today, with improved harmony in the United Nations, it is doubtful that an effort to conclude a sanctions convention would be successful. But it is worth considering whether an effort outside the United Nations, involving the United States and other like-minded states, would be worthwhile.

A Modest Proposal

Keith Highet, a former president of the American Society of International Law, has made a provocative proposal for a Draft Convention for the Suppression of State-Sponsored Terrorism to the organization's Committee on Responses to State-Sponsored Terrorism.[24] Highet's proposal raises definitional issues addressed earlier in this book, as well as a host of other legal and political concerns. With respect to the definition of "terrorism" or the "proscribed act"—and in accordance with the functional approach suggested earlier—the draft convention would be applicable only to attacks against "unarmed or innocent civilians" if a series of other conditions were met. But this limitation would leave military personnel and government officials highly vulnerable to terrorist attacks, as would the limitation that the victim be "unconnected with any governmental or other authority." Excluded, for example, would be the murder of U.S. Navy diver Robert Stethem on the hijacked TWA 847 flight. Also, the term "innocent" is inherently ambiguous and could result in prolonged debates in application. Accordingly, I would revise Highet's definition of a "proscribed act" to read:

(1) *an act of violence* committed as a political threat or demonstration;
    (a) unrelated to a sustained and organized military action;
    (b) aimed deliberately or recklessly, at
    (c) unarmed persons, who are

(d) killed or seriously injured as a result of the act of violence, when:

(2) *the act occurs*
    (a) on the territory of a signatory State, or
    (b) in an airplane or vessel of its registry, or
    (c) against the person of any unarmed person who is a national thereof.

As to definition of sponsorship, Highet introduced the innovative concept (which I support) of holding a state responsible when it applauds the commission of narrowly defined terrorist acts. This is directed, of course, toward Libya's initial praise (later recanted) for the terrorist attacks at the Rome and Vienna airports in 1985. A state lauding behavior that decent-minded people would find morally reprehensible cannot be classified as an exercise of freedom of speech. To the contrary, when issued under official state authority, such a statement constitutes incitement to an international crime.

I also support Highet's concept of a special tribunal to determine (in camera if necessary to protect intelligence sources) whether a state has sponsored terrorism. If this tribunal were composed of senior respected jurists, as Highet suggests, the impartiality of the decision would lend a substantial measure of credibility to any determination that a state had sponsored terrorism.

Highet's proposal envisages the imposition of draconian sanctions—in his words, a state determined to be sponsoring terrorism would be subject to a kind of "civil death" in international law. Sweeping sanctions of the kind proposed by Highet would go much further than any multilateral sanctions have gone in the past. The question therefore arises whether there is any practical possibility, now or in the foreseeable future, of agreement on such a proposal. Highet has "no illusions" about the difficulties involved in getting even like-minded states to agree. He notes further, however, that

> The modest proposal now being presented . . . sets aside these obvious practical and political difficulties and does so on purpose. It proceeds on the theory—which may be mistaken, but which has not really been argued—that even though we are not there yet, at the present rate we are going to be at a juncture in perhaps 10 or 15 years where there is sufficient consensus to implement measures against a sponsoring

State in the form of an international agreement, and that we should therefore start facing up to the realities now. It also proceeds on the theory that having a previously agreed menu of possible common actions, and a standing mechanism for determining a "sponsor" State's responsibility, may make a political consensus easier to achieve than would otherwise be the case. Finally, it proceeds on the theory that the particular structure of the proposal is such that once two States have entered into agreement, there will be an incentive for others, within a predetermined group of potential parties (*e.g.,* the OECD countries) to join the group. Most will not wish to be "outside the pale" for long.

One might also examine the reasons European states have been unwilling to impose sweeping sanctions and consider what, if anything, might be done to overcome this reluctance. A commonly identified obstacle is the economic cost to the states imposing the sanctions. States with substantial economic ties to a state sponsoring terrorism will weigh this factor carefully before agreeing to sanctions. A possible way to minimize, if not overcome, the economic cost factor would be for the United States and like-minded states to agree on an arrangement whereby those states that would suffer the most severe economic costs in imposing sanctions could have these burdens relieved by compensatory payments from other states participating in the sanctions. Article 50 of the United Nations Charter may serve as a partial guide in this respect:

> If preventive or enforcement measures against any state are taken by the Security Council, any other state, whether a Member of the United Nations or not, which finds itself confronted with special economic problems arising from the carrying out of those measures shall have the right to consult the Security Council with regard to a solution of those problems.

Another model might be the burden-sharing arrangements that have been developed by the International Energy Agency for use in the event of another oil crisis.[25] Here as there the goal would be an equitable sharing of burdens in the common interest.

Political factors also may constitute a substantial barrier to sanctions. Syria's influence in the Middle East—the perception that it will play a pivotal role in any peaceful settlement of the Arab-Israeli conflict—has been cited as a reason for the resistance to imposing harsh sanctions against it. But there are recent indications that even the relatively mild sanctions imposed against Syria after evidence produced by various sources demonstrated conclusively its sponsorship of terrorism have caused Syria to rethink its position.[26] Sanctions in this instance at least seem to have had beneficial effect.

An advantage of Highet's proposal is that it would put potential state sponsors of terrorism on notice that they would be incurring substantial risk were they to put their plans into action. The draft convention would also represent a statement by a significant segment of the world community that certain acts are morally impermissible under any circumstances and that state sponsorship of them will entail serious consequences. As Highet suggests, it may not be currently possible to make such a statement in the form of a binding convention, but it may be worthwhile to start the process toward such an approach in the hope that in the not-too-distant future it may come to fruition.

There can be little doubt that even the threat, much less the imposition, of the sanctions suggested by the Highet proposal would likely be more effective than unilateral sanctions employed by the United States or U.S. sanctions modestly supported by its allies. Besides avoiding the many difficulties associated with unilateral U.S. actions—such as controversies over their "extraterritorial" application—multilateral sanctions, applied automatically if certain criteria were met, would greatly enhance the possibility of fulfilling the goals of economic sanctions against states sponsoring terrorism.

These goals, which have recently been identified and discussed by Professor Kenneth Abbott,[27] include (1) economic warfare; (2) imposing costs; (3) denial of means; and (4) symbolic communication. As Abbott points out, the United States has apparently not yet come to view its imposition of economic sanctions against states sponsoring terrorism as an exercise in economic warfare. Highet's proposed sanctions, however, could be so viewed. They would serve to underscore the seriousness with which the sanctioning states view state sponsorship of terrorism.

Imposing costs has been a primary goal of U.S. economic sanctions and would be a major objective of the sanctions offered by Highet. Moreover, the cost to the target state of these sanctions would be much more substantial than the costs any state sponsoring terrorism has previously had to bear. In most cases, the United States has had few economic links it could sever with states sponsoring terrorism. Widely applied multilateral sanctions, however, would involve the cutting of substantial economic ties with the target state, many of them of crucial importance to that state's economy. These would not be economic costs the target state could suffer with equanimity.

With respect to denial of means, Abbott notes that this goal may be fulfilled if the intent of the sanctions is to limit conventional military capabilities. Economic sanctions have little effect in denying states the means to sponsor terrorism, however, because most terrorist acts are carried out through the use of small arms, ordinary explosives, and similar weapons. These are available from a variety of sources other than the states that would be parties to the draft convention.

Abbott stresses that recent scholarship has emphasized the importance of symbolic communication as a goal of economic sanctions. He illustrates his support for this view by reference to "some of the messages the United States appears to have communicated by strengthening economic sanctions against Syria in November 1986."[28] According to Abbott, several messages were sent to Syria:

> [T]hey conveyed determination, commitment to the goal of opposing state supported terrorism and an intention to take action in support of that goal. An action like the imposition of sanctions conveys these messages more credibly than mere words because it demonstrates that the United States is willing to bear costs and to accept risks in pursuit of its goals. By imposing sanctions, after all, the United States loses gains from trade, acquires a reputation as an unreliable supplier, and incurs the risk that Syria will cause harm to hostages held by terrorist groups it supports, sabotage the Middle East peace process or use force against Israel or respond in other damaging ways. Sanctions can also communicate a threat of military action. The embargo of Libya was clearly designed to convey such a threat; the sanctions against Syria, in contrast, were not.[29]

At the same time, Abbott notes, the relatively moderate nature of the sanctions the United States imposed against Syria "made clear that it [the United States] did not want to provoke a military or political reaction that might be worse than Syria's support of terrorism."[30] The United States also made it clear that it was keeping the door open for a change of heart on Syria's part and for the possibility of cooperation for mutual interests. This message seemed to have some impact because in June 1987 Syria closed the office of the Abu Nidal organization, made efforts to secure the release of Western hostages held in Lebanon, and apparently has recently refrained from sponsoring terrorist activities.[31]

Were Highet's proposal for a Draft Convention for the Suppression of State-Sponsored Terrorism to be implemented, it would send some very strong symbolic communications indeed. Such a convention would be an extremely important confirmation of the impermissibility of state-sponsored terrorism and would put states on notice that they risked the imposition of severe sanctions by their actions. It would also send a message to states other than potential target states that the states parties to the convention were determined to deal with this problem and that these other states should join them in this effort. The convention would demonstrate convincingly the willingness of the parties to pay the costs of these sanctions and to share these costs equitably. Last, it would demonstrate the resolve of the states that are parties to settle disputes peacefully and to avoid, if at all possible, the resort to armed force, the subject of the next chapter.

Notes

1. For an authoritative discussion of such sanctions, see A. LOWENFELD, TRADE CONTROLS FOR POLITICAL ENDS (2d ed. 1983).

2. For an exhaustive review of these statutes and others relating to the president's ability to use economic sanctions, *see* B. CARTER, INTERNATIONAL ECONOMIC SANCTIONS: IMPROVING THE HAPHAZARD U.S. LEGAL REGIME (1988); *see also* U.S. Department of State, *Economic Sanctions to Combat International Terrorism,* Bureau of Public Affairs Special Report No. 149, July 1986, at 1.

3. Perhaps the most sharply critical study and the article generally regarded as the landmark on the subject of export controls is Berman and Garson, *United States Export Controls—Past, Present and Future,* 67 COLUM. L. REV. 791 (1967). For a more recent study, also critical of the effectiveness of economic sanctions, *see* M. DAUODI & M. DAJANI, ECONOMIC SANCTIONS 43–48, 178–188 (1983).

4. *See, e.g.,* G. HUFBAUER & J. SCHOTT, ECONOMIC SANCTIONS RECONSIDERED: HISTORY AND CURRENT POLICY (1985); Bialos & Juster, *The Libyan Sanctions: A Rational Response to State-Sponsored Terrorism,* 26 VA. J. INT'L L. 799 (1986); Abbott, *Economic Sanctions and International Terrorism,* 20 VAND. J. TRANSNAT'L L. 289 (1987); Abbott, *Coercion and Communication: Frameworks for Evaluation of Economic Sanctions,* 19 N.Y.U.J. INT'L L. & POL. 781 (1987).

5. For an extensive discussion of these sanctions, *see* Malloy, *The Iran Crisis: Law Under Pressure,* 1984 WIS. INT'L L.J. 15.

6. Exec. Order No. 12,543, 51 Fed. Reg. 865 (1986).

7. *See* 15 C.F.R. § 385.4(d) (1987) for the current regulation on these sanctions.

8. For a description of the sanctions the United States imposed in 1986, see U.S. Takes Measures Against Syria, White House Statement, Nov. 14, 1986, *reprinted in* 87 DEP'T STATE BULL. 79 (Jan. 1987). For the sanctions imposed in June 1987, *see* 52 Fed. Reg. 23,167, 23,168 (June 18, 1987) (renumbering 15 C.F.R. § 385.4(d)(4) and § 385.4(d)(5) and adding a new § 385.4(d)(4)).

9. Bonn Declaration on Hijacking of 1978, *reprinted in* 17 I.L.M. 1285 (1978).

10. *See* Chamberlain, *Collective Suspension of Air Services with States Which Harbour Hijackers,* 32 INT'L & COMP. L.Q. 616, 627 (1983).

11. *Id.*

12. 81 DEP'T STATE BULL. 16 (1981).

13. Chamberlain, *supra* note 10, at 628.

14. *Id.*

15. The following discussion draws heavily on G.M. LEVITT, DEMOCRACIES AGAINST TERROR: THE WESTERN RESPONSE TO STATE-SUPPORTED TERRORISM (1988).

16. *Id.* at 5.

17. N.Y. Times, June 30, 1985, at A1, col. 4.

18. LEVITT, *supra* note 15, at 59.

19. *Id.* at 63–64.

20. *See Combatting International and Domestic Terrorism: Hearings on S. 2236 Before the Senate Comm. on Foreign Relations,* 95th Cong., 2d Sess. (1978).

21. S. 1282, introduced on July 28, 1987.

22. See Bremer, *Counterterrorism: U.S. Policy and Proposed Legislation,* 88 DEP'T STATE BULL. 44, 46–47 (Jan. 1988).

23. For a discussion of these efforts, *see* Chamberlain, *supra* note 10.

24. In 1986 Keith Highet, president of the American Society of International Law, appointed a Committee on Responses to State-Sponsored Terrorism. The committee, which I chair, includes the following members:

Yoram Dinstein, professor of law, Tel-Aviv University, Israel; L.F.E. Goldie, professor of law, Syracuse University; Richard A. Falk, Albert G. Milbank Professor of International Law and Practice, Princeton University; Robert H. Kupperman, Center for Strategic and International Studies, Georgetown University; Richard B. Lillich, Howard W. Smith, professor of law, University of Virginia Law School; Roberts B. Owen, Esq., Covington & Burling, Washington, D.C.; Eugene V. Rostow, professor of law, National Defense University; and Louis B. Sohn, Woodruff Professor of International Law, University of Georgia. Keith Highet and John Lawrence Hargrove, executive director of the American Society of International Law, serve as *ex officio* members of the committee. John H. McNeill, assistant general counsel for international affairs, Department of Defense, serves as resource person for the committee.

25. For a discussion of this arrangement, *see* Murphy, *The International Energy Program: An Assessment,* 26 DE PAUL L. REV. 595, 604–609 (1977).

26. *See* Bremer, *supra* note 22, at 46.

27. *See* Abbott, *Economic Sanctions and International Terrorism, supra* note 4, at 300–24.

28. *Id.* at 319.

29. *Id.* at 319–20.

30. *Id.* at 321.

31. See Bremer, *supra* note 22, at 46.

6

The Use of Armed Force

In this chapter we turn to the most coercive—and the most controversial—response to international terrorism: the use of armed force. There are two major types of armed-force responses. The first, rescue missions, is directed specifically against the terrorists and is designed for the direct benefit of the victims of the terrorist act. The second, actions against supporting or sponsoring states, raises a different set of legal issues. As we shall see, it is at times extremely difficult to distinguish between the two types.

Rescue Missions

The two rescue missions of victims of terrorism that best illustrate the relevant legal issues are the Israeli rescue actions at Entebbe, Uganda, and the abortive U.S. attempt to free the Americans held hostage in Teheran, Iran. The Entebbe incident, in particular, may be regarded as the classic case.

The Israeli Rescue at Entebbe

The salient facts of the Israeli rescue at the Entebbe airport at Uganda may be briefly summarized as follows.[1] On June 27, 1976, four terrorists, members of the Popular Front for the Liberation of Palestine, a splinter group of the PLO, took control of an Air France jet shortly after it had taken off from the Athens airport. The hijackers first flew their hostages to Benghazi, Libya, for refueling and then to Entebbe airport in Uganda, where they were held for six days in an unused passenger terminal. Israeli discussions with President Idi Amin of Uganda, as well as intelligence reports and other sources of information, indicated quite conclusively that not only was President Amin not making efforts to free the hostages and apprehend the hijackers, but he was actively involved in support of the hijacking operation.

There was substantial objective evidence of Uganda's active support. When the aircraft landed in Entebbe, 6 Palestinians, members of one or more divisions of the PLO, joined the hijackers, and Ugandan soldiers assisted in the surveillance of the hostages. Shortly after the plane landed at Entebbe, the hijackers demanded that 53 prisoners be released (40 incarcerated in Israel, the other 13 elsewhere). President Amin informed the hostages that the hijackers held no grudge against them, but "only against the fascist Israeli government—and if the latter does not agree to the guerrillas' demands, it does not care about the fate of its citizens."[2] The next day all Israelis were segregated in another part of the airport. On June 30, 47 non-Israeli women and children were released and allowed to go to Paris, and the following day 100 French hostages were released and allowed to leave the country. The 96 Israelis remained at Entebbe under the guard of the hijackers, who were relieved from time to time by Ugandan armed forces.

As evidence mounted of the futility of attempts to resolve the problem diplomatically, the Israeli government decided to go ahead with a military raid on Entebbe in an effort to rescue the Israeli hostages. On July 3, under cover of darkness, three planeloads of Israeli commandos made a surprise landing at the Entebbe airfield and within less than an hour were airborne with the remaining Israeli hostages. In the course of the raid, 1 Israeli soldier, 3 hostages, 20 Ugandan soldiers, and apparently all of the hijackers were killed. An uncertain number of other persons were wounded. Ten Ugandan aircraft were destroyed, and considerable damage was done to various parts of the airfield. One Israeli woman, who had been taken to a Ugandan hospital earlier in the week, had to be left behind; she apparently was murdered by Ugandan soldiers in retaliation for the raid. After the plane stopped in Nairobi to refuel and to carry out emergency surgery on the wounded—at least the tacit consent of the Kenya government to do so had been secured in advance—the hostages arrived back in Israel Sunday morning, exactly a week after their takeoff from Athens.

Five days after the raid on Entebbe, the Organization of African Unity (OAU) submitted a complaint to the United Nations Security Council charging "an act of aggression" by Israel against Uganda. Not surprisingly, the OAU's version of the facts regarding the raid differed sharply from those just set forth. The foreign minister of Uganda, Juma Oris Abdalla, and the representative of Mauritania, Moulaye El Hassen, speaking on behalf of the African group, argued that the Israeli raid constituted aggression under article 2(4) of the UN Charter because it had violated the territorial sovereignty and political independence of a member of the United Nations. According to their version of the facts, not only was the government of Uganda innocent of any collusion with the hijackers, but it was making every effort, in cooperation with other governments and the secretary-general, to obtain the freedom of the hostages. Further, they contended that these efforts were leading to a peaceful resolution of the problem when Israel decided "to take the law into its own hands." Thus, they argued, the council should adopt a draft resolution (introduced by Benin, Libya, and Tanzania) condemning Israel's flagrant violation of Uganda's sovereignty and territorial integrity and demanding that Israel meet the just claims of Uganda for full compensation for the damage and destruction inflicted on it.

In response, the Israeli ambassador to the United Nations, Chaim Herzog, sharply disputed Uganda's version of the facts, repeatedly stressing evidence of Uganda's collaboration with the hijackers and of the imminent danger to the Israeli hostages. On the basis of this version of the events, Herzog turned to a defense of the raid at Entebbe under principles of international law. He first contended that Uganda had violated a basic tenet of customary international law by failing to protect foreign nationals on its territory. He further argued that Uganda's actions constituted a "gross violation" of the 1970 Hague Convention for the Suppression of Unlawful Seizure of Aircraft, which both Israel and Uganda had signed and ratified. Specifically, Herzog claimed Uganda had violated the following articles of the Hague Convention:

Article 6: Upon being satisfied that the circumstances so warrant, any Contracting State in the territory of which the offender or the alleged offender is present, shall take him into custody or take other measures to ensure his presence. The custody and other measure shall

be as provided in the law of that State but may only be continued
for such time as is necessary to enable any criminal or extradition
proceedings to be instituted.

Article 7: The Contracting State in the territory of which the
alleged offender is found shall, if it does not extradite him, be obliged,
without exception whatsoever and whether or not the offence was
committed in its territory, to submit the case to its competent authorities
for the purpose of prosecution. Those authorities shall take their
decision in the same manner as in the case of any ordinary offence
of a serious nature under the law of that State.

Article 9: When any of the acts . . . has occurred or is about to
occur, Contracting States shall take all appropriate measures to restore
control of the aircraft to its lawful commander or to preserve his
control of the aircraft. In cases contemplated . . . , any Contracting
State in which the aircraft or its passengers and crew are present
shall facilitate the continuation of the journey of the passengers and
crew as soon as practicable, and shall without delay return the aircraft
and its cargo to the persons lawfully entitled to possession.

Herzog did not claim that these violations of customary and
conventional international law by themselves justified Israel's use of
armed force on Ugandan territory. Rather, in this regard he stressed
two primary lines of argument: First, he contended that Israel's raid
did not violate article 2(4) of the Charter because that provision
does not "prohibit a use of force which is limited in intention and
effect to the protection of a State's own integrity and its nationals'
vital interests, when the machinery envisaged by the United Nations
Charter is ineffective in the situation."[3] Second, he invoked the right
of a state under the doctrine of self-defense to take military action
to protect its nationals in mortal danger provided such action is
limited to cases that present no other means to protect threatened
nationals and secure their safe removal. In Herzog's view, the situation
at Entebbe was in complete accord with the classic formulation of
a "necessity of self-defence, instant, overwhelming, leaving no choice
of means and no moment for deliberation."[4]

Herzog pointed to a precedent: France's use of force just a few
months before the raid at Entebbe in order to rescue a busload of
children held hostage on the Somalia border. The representatives
of the terrorists in Somalia had announced that if their demands
on the French government were not met, they would cut the children's

throats. In response, French soldiers attacked the terrorists, killing them and rescuing the children, except for one child who was killed by the terrorists and one child who was taken to Somalia but later returned alive. During the attack, French soldiers were fired at from a Somalia frontier post, and a French lieutenant was seriously wounded. The French forces returned the fire, causing casualties and property damage. Although Somalia complained about the incident in the Security Council, it received little support, and the council took no formal action.

The United States strongly supported the legality of the Israeli raid at Entebbe, but it did so cautiously. In the Security Council debate, U.S. Ambassador William Scranton "reaffirmed" the principle of territorial sovereignty in Africa. He also stated that Israel's breach of the territorial integrity of Uganda, although short in duration and only temporary, would normally be impermissible under the United Nations Charter. However, according to Scranton, the situation at Entebbe involved "unique circumstances," which it was hoped would not arise again in the future. In his words:

> [T]here is a well-established right to use limited force for the protection of one's own nationals from an imminent threat of injury or death in a situation where the state in whose territory they are located either is unwilling or unable to protect them. The right, flowing from the right of self-defense, is limited to such use of force as is necessary and appropriate to protect threatened nationals from injury.
>
> The requirements of this right to protect nationals were clearly met in the Entebbe case. Israel had good reason to believe that at the time it acted Israeli nationals were in imminent danger of execution by the hijackers. Moreover, the actions necessary to release the Israeli nationals or to prevent substantial loss of Israeli lives had not been taken by the Government of Uganda, nor was there a reasonable expectation such actions would be taken. In fact, there is substantial evidence that the Government of Uganda cooperated with and aided the hijackers.
>
> A number of the released hostages have publicly related how the Ugandan authorities allowed several additional terrorists to reinforce the original group after the plane landed, permitted them to receive additional arms and additional explosives, participated in guarding the hostages, and according to some accounts, even took over sole custody of some or all of the passengers to allow the hijackers to rest.

The ease and success of the Israeli effort to free the hostages further suggests that the Ugandan authorities could have overpowered the hijackers and released the hostages if they had really had the desire to do so.[5]

Ambassador Scranton also emphasized the reasonableness of Israel's conclusion that the hostages were in imminent danger of execution, since the Ugandan government was headed by an individual who had previously rejoiced at the slaying of Israeli athletes at Munich, who had called for the extinction of Israel, and who had praised Hitler's slaughter of six million Jews.

After four days of debate, the Security Council failed to take any formal action. On July 14 the United States and the United Kingdom introduced a resolution by which the Security Council would have condemned hijacking and all other acts that threatened the lives of passengers and crews and the safety of international civil aviation and called on all states to take every necessary measure to prevent and punish all such terrorist acts. Under the resolution, the council would also have deplored the tragic loss of human life that had resulted from the hijacking of French aircraft; reaffirmed the need to respect the sovereignty and territorial integrity of all states in accordance with the United Nations Charter and international law; and enjoined the international community to give the highest priority to the consideration of further means of assuring the safety and reliability of international civil aviation. The resolution failed to obtain the necessary majority of the fifteen member states. The vote was six in favor, none against, with two abstentions.[6] (The draft resolution sponsored by Benin, Libya, and Tanzania was not pressed to a vote.)

In a statement made after the vote on the U.S.-UK resolution, the U.S. representative, Ambassador W. Tapley Bennett, expressed his delegation's regret that the council had declined to take positive action against the hijacking of the Air France airliner, but he expressed satisfaction that "not a single delegation could bring itself to vote against such a balanced resolution."[7] He again stressed that the "sovereignty and territorial integrity of states must be sustained and protected." Specifically, he emphasized that the United States did not view the raid "as a precedent which would justify any future unauthorized entry into another state's territory that is not similarly justified by exceptional circumstances."[8]

Implications for Future Action. As just described, the United States—and to a somewhat lesser extent, Israel—adopted an extremely cautious approach in defense of the legality of the raid at Entebbe. U.S. representatives repeatedly stressed the need to protect and sustain the sovereignty and territorial integrity of states; the "exceptional," indeed "unique," circumstances present at Entebbe; and the doctrine of self-defense of a state's nationals abroad as the primary, if not the sole, justification for the Israeli use of armed force. This approach appears eminently sound in law and policy. The incident at Entebbe was exceptional because of the congruence of a number of factors that, the best evidence indicates, were present there:

1. The active involvement of President Amin in, at a minimum, the last stages of the hijacking operation
2. The lack of any indications that steps would be taken by Ugandan authorities to secure the release of the Israeli hostages
3. The Israeli officials' reasonable perception that the hostages were in imminent danger of execution by the hijackers, perhaps with the active participation of Ugandan soldiers
4. Israel's consequent—and reasonable—conclusion that military action was urgently required by the exigencies of the situation
5. The limitation by the Israeli military of the use of force to the minimum necessary to accomplish the rescue and the swift termination of the use of force upon completion of the mission
6. The absence of any punitive motive on the part of Israel toward Uganda and the limited loss of life and property caused by the raid
7. The acquiescence of the Kenyan government in the refueling of the Israeli planes at the Nairobi airport

The cautious approach taken by the U.S. government in its defense of the raid at Entebbe is especially noteworthy, because some prominent authorities on international law have been much less restrained in their defense of the raid. In a letter to the editor of the *New*

York Times, Myres McDougal and Michael Reisman defended the raid along the following lines:

There is a bizarre Newspeak quality to the denunciations, in terms of asserted international law, of the Israeli rescue of hijacked passengers from the Entebbe airport in Uganda on July 4.

The initial act of air piracy at Athens was a violation of international law, as was the holding of the hostages for political purposes thereafter. At least one of these acts, piracy, is an international crime subject to universal jurisdiction.

The Israeli action would appear justified as a humanitarian intervention, a doctrine whose roots go back, at least, to Hugo Grotius. Where gross violations of human rights are taking place within a state whose government will not or cannot prevent them, the organs of the international community, or in exigent circumstances a single state, may enter the territory of the defaulting state for the sole purpose of terminating the outrage.

This act is recognized as a lawful humanitarian intervention. For a detailed exploration of the historical application and deep roots in common interest of this doctrine see our "Memorandum on Humanitarian Intervention to Save the Ibos," reprinted in Lillich, "Humanitarian Intervention" (1973).

Another hallowed doctrine of international law, availing Israel in this case and expressing in many forms the common interests of all peoples, is that of "self-help." The forms of this doctrine include self-defense, reprisals, retaliation, impact territoriality, contiguous zones and other equivalents. The core meaning is that if a state is grievously injured but the organized international community is incapable of affording timely redress, the injured party may take necessary and proportionate measures to protect itself and its nationals.

In a context of the most inhumane deprivations and the failure of the Ugandan Government to give protection, it can only be Opposite-speak to describe the rescue operation as an act of aggression against Uganda. The action of the Israelis could not possibly have had the effect of threatening the territorial integrity or political independence of Uganda. This action, on the contrary, was entirely necessary and proportionate to the lawful purposes of the rescue.

The suggestion that, under the circumstances, Israel's action was an invasion of the sovereignty of Uganda involves a complete misunderstanding of sovereignty. Sovereignty even in its most comprehensive conception refers only to that competence of states which international law confers. States are not accorded a competence to exclude themselves from the operative provisions of international law.

It is regrettable that states and international organizations fail to censure the Amin regime. One can only wonder at the Security Council's curious strabismus in focusing righteously on the wrong problem.[9]

With all due respect to the prominence of these writers, I view this letter in effect as an advocate's brief—it should not serve as a guide to the use of armed force as a measure of self-help, either for the U.S. government or for other states in the world community. The writers list self-defense as only one of numerous measures of "self-help" involving the use of force, all of which (at least as far as can be inferred from the letter) remain fully available to states in spite of the strict limits on the use of force imposed by the United Nations Charter. Especially disturbing if intended as a possible guide to future state action is the writers' sentence: "The core meaning [of the doctrine of self-help] is that if a state is grievously injured but the organized international community is incapable of affording timely redress, the injured party may take necessary and proportionate measures to protect itself and its nationals." This sentence is pregnant with ambiguity: "Grievously injured" is strikingly imprecise phraseology to describe a situation in which a state should be deemed justified under international law to resort to the unilateral use of armed force, even if this response is required to be "necessary and proportionate" (terms themselves not free of ambiguity) to the injury inflicted.

The writers' primary rationale for justification for the Israeli raid appears to be the so-called doctrine of humanitarian intervention, but the historical record reveals few if any genuine cases of this legal theory.[10] It is also highly debatable whether this doctrine remains viable in light of the United Nations Charter's limitations on the use of force and the Organization of American States (OAS) charter's strict prohibitions on intervention for any purpose whatsoever.[11] I favor the position taken by Thomas Franck, who holds that the doctrine of humanitarian intervention is incompatible with principles of modern public international law. But Franck is also correct when he states:

Yet we freely admit that we can imagine situations in which a humanitarian rescue would be highly desirable. With Churchill, we can visualize wanting our country to fight the menace of tyranny for years, and if necessary alone. Undeniably, there are circumstances in which the unilateral use of force to overthrow injustice begins to seem less wrong than to turn aside. Like civil disobedience, however, this sense of superior necessity belongs in the realm not of law but of moral choice, which nations, like individuals, must sometimes make, weighing the costs and benefits to their cause, to the social fabric, and to themselves.[12]

The raid on Entebbe did not present the difficult choice envisaged by Franck; the doctrine of self-defense afforded a solid legal as well as moral basis for the action.

Variations on a Theme: Entebbe Revisited. As noted in the preceding section, the primary justification advanced in the Security Council in support of the raid on Entebbe was Israel's right to protect its nationals, a right that Ambassador Scranton said flowed from the right of self-defense. The question to be addressed here is whether the crucial factor supporting permissibility was the fact that Israeli nationals were involved. For example, if the hostages at Entebbe had been nationals of Kenya (or some other third country), could Israel legitimately have carried out the raid?

My conclusion is that Israel could have taken such action, at least if it had been requested to do so by Kenya or the other states whose nationals were endangered. The legal rationale for this action would be the doctrine of collective self-defense—an admittedly complex and controversial doctrine, the very existence of which has been challenged by some jurists.[13] Others have claimed that it can be employed only in accordance with the terms of mutual security pacts such as the North Atlantic Treaty Organization (NATO),[14] or in the absence of such pacts, only by states in geographical proximity.[15] Both of these proposed limitations seem artificial; neither serves policy. The entire world community has an interest in protecting innocent individuals from acts of international terrorism. The fact that a particular state does not have the military means to defend its nationals abroad in a situation in which another state is actively collaborating with terrorists should not preclude the weak state from calling on countries that do have the necessary military capabilities for assistance. As Myres McDougal and Florentino Feliciano have suggested, in this situation each member of the world community "in effect asserts, singly and in combination, defense of the new and more comprehensive 'self.'"[16] Mutual security pacts such as NATO were not designed with individual acts of international terrorism in mind and are therefore entirely inapposite to the problem. Moreover, in an age of global communications and travel, geographic proximity would seem an irrelevant consideration for purposes of determining the permissible scope of collective self-defense.

An analogy has been drawn by Derek Bowett to national law principles of self-defense. Writing in 1958, he noted that the common law recognized self-defense as extending beyond the defense of one's own person or property, but that there had to be some close relationship between the person attacked and the person who assists in his lawful defense. That is, the so-called defense of others was limited to those who were members of one's household, or those whom one was under a legal or socially recognized duty to protect.[17] However, more recent cases and commentators recognize the artificiality of these limitations and "recognize the privilege of the defendant to defend a third person against any kind of invasion against which the third person would have the privilege of self-defense, so long as the intervention appeared to be reasonably necessary."[18] For these reasons, such an approach should apply a fortiori at the international level.

Two other variations of the situation at Entebbe may be briefly mentioned. First, assume the evidence indicated that the government of Uganda was not actively collaborating with the hijackers but was unable to exercise its responsibility to protect the hostages and that the execution of the hostages by the hijackers was imminent. If all other facts of the Entebbe raid remained unchanged, the raid could still be justified under the doctrine of self-defense. As Humphrey Waldock has written:

> The landing of forces without consent, being unmistakably a usurpation of political authority, is prima facie intervention. The question is whether it satisfied the principles laid down in the Caroline incident. There must be (1) an imminent threat of injury to nationals, (2) a failure or inability on the part of the territorial sovereign to protect

them and (3) measures of protection strictly confined to the object
of protecting them against injury. Even under customary law only an
absolute necessity could justify an intervention to protect nationals.
But, where such necessity existed, intervention seems to have been
legally justifiable in the period before the Covenant [of the League
of Nations].[19]

Second, there would seem to be no question of the legality of
the Israeli raid had it been made with the consent of the Ugandan
government. It is a generally recognized principle of international
law that a state may intervene in the internal affairs of another
state at the request of that country's lawful government.[20] (It may
be noted, however, that questions have arisen with respect to past
interventions—most particularly the U.S.-Belgian airdrop into the
Congo [Stanleyville] in 1964 and the U.S. action in the Dominican
Republic in 1965—as to whether the invitation came from the
government legitimately in power and whether the use of armed
force was solely for the purpose of protecting foreign nationals or
was employed to keep the requesting government in power in a
situation in which a state of belligerency existed requiring neutrality
of outside powers.[21]) Presumably, no such questions would have arisen
in connection with an Israeli intervention authorized by the Ugandan
government.

U.S. Rescue Attempt in the Iranian Hostage Crisis

Israel's success at Entebbe was not matched by the United States
in its effort on April 24, 1980, to rescue U.S. American diplomats
held hostage in Teheran. The U.S. rescue attempt was aborted in
the Iranian desert when eight Americans died in the fire resulting
from a collision between a refueler plane and one of the helicopters.
Although no hostages died in the incident, their captivity continued
for another nine months.[22]

The U.S. rescue attempt raises many of the same issues involved
in Israeli action at Entebbe, which have been explored in other
forums, especially by Professor Oscar Schachter.[23] The two situations,
however, have some differences that raise additional issues of law
and policy.

For example, the U.S. rescue attempt occurred five months after the seizure of the U.S. Embassy in Teheran. Many efforts had been made in the United Nations and through various intermediaries to secure release of the hostages. The International Court of Justice had issued an interim order demanding their release.[24] Unilateral economic sanctions had been imposed against Iran by the United States. None of these and other measures had produced any significant change in the Iranian position. The ICJ's decision on the merits was still pending at the time of the rescue attempt.[25] Under these circumstances could it be said that the United States had failed to exhaust all pacific means of settlement under articles 2(3) and 33 of the UN Charter? More broadly, must all pacific means of settlement be exhausted before force may be legitimately employed?

As suggested by Schachter, the answer would appear to be clearly "no," if the lives of the hostages are in imminent danger or even if the government of which they are nationals reasonably perceives them to be in such danger. In Schachter's words:

Were the hostages actually in imminent peril in April 1980? That question is probably not answerable even today. The pertinent point is whether at the time, the U.S. government had reason to fear that in the emotional atmosphere of Iranian revolutionary ferment the hostages would be executed, with or without a trial. As a general rule, it seems reasonable to recognize that the state whose nationals are imprisoned as hostages should have wide latitude to make the decision whether they are in extreme danger. In effect this would place the burden on the state responsible for the illegal act of hostage-taking to demonstrate that the hostages are not in grave danger. They might do this by assurances made publicly and to international organs and by placing the hostages under the authority and control of disciplined military or police units. This was not the case in Iran. Verbal attacks and threats against the hostages were made by prominent figures and custody was exercised by emotional "militants." Fears as to the safety of the hostages were an inevitable reaction. The fact that negotiations later proved successful does not show that these fears lacked plausibility.

The conclusion, therefore, is that regardless of whether or not the hostages were actually in extreme danger, the conditions were such as to lead the U.S. government to believe that they were. Faced with this fact and the not unrealistic conclusion at the time that peaceful means offered no promise of release, the United States had reasonable grounds to consider a military action as necessary to effect a rescue. On these premises, the action taken did not violate the Charter or international law. Whether or not the rescue action was wise in a political and military sense is of course a different matter.[26]

Other comments by Schachter, however, raise more complex questions:

> By changing the facts a little another question is sharpened. Suppose hostages are taken and a demand is made for concessions by the state of which they are nationals (whether or not diplomats). Assume that the hostages are neither subjected to threats nor are they ill-treated. There is no indication that their lives are in danger. Should force be allowed on the ground that hostage-taking is in itself an "act which endangers innocent human lives," as stated in the preamble of the Convention on the Taking of Hostages (1979)? The answer to this, I would suggest, must depend on whether the hostages are in fact in imminent danger. The illegality of their detention and the failure of international organs to obtain their release should not be enough to legitimize the use of force to effectuate their release. To allow the use of force in the absence of imminent peril would imply a "necessity" to use force to redress a legal wrong. It would be significantly different from the necessity of self-defense to repel an attack or to save lives.[27]

Schachter's position is in general correct, although the question remains of how far it should be extended. Should the legality of an attempt to rescue hostages always be dependent upon a finding or at least a reasonable perception that their lives are in imminent danger? If all possible means of peaceful settlement are exhausted and yet the hostage takers indicate that they are willing to keep the hostages into the indefinite future until such time as their demands are met, would the state of which the hostages are nationals be prohibited from resorting to armed force?

Schachter is accurate in stating that the rules of article 2(3) and article 2(4) of the UN Charter may not be disregarded merely because a state finds it necessary to vindicate a legal right. But it does not necessarily follow that armed force may not be used to save hostages from an indefinite detention when all other means have proven futile. In such a case, it would appear necessary to use force to protect the hostages from serious injury. Although their lives might not be in jeopardy, their psychological and physical well-being—to say nothing of their fundamental liberties—would be greatly threatened. Indefinite incarceration of a state's nationals should be regarded as a continuing armed attack giving rise to a right on the part of that state to use force under article 51 of the UN Charter.

The key issue in each case would be the *necessity* of the use of armed force. The burden of proof, moreover, would be on the state resorting to armed force. To meet this burden in a situation in which the hostages' lives were not in imminent peril, the state resorting to armed force would have to demonstrate that all possible means of peaceful settlement had been exhausted—or that to resort to them would be futile. No such showing would be necessary if hostages' lives were in imminent peril, the hostage takers had indicated an intent to detain the hostages indefinitely until demands were met, and the armed force used was limited to the amount necessary to rescue the hostages and did not constitute a punitive reprisal.

Armed Force Against States Supporting or Sponsoring Terrorism

This section focuses on the use of armed force against states rather than against the terrorists themselves. In doing so, it uses the definitional approach discussed previously in distinguishing between states that support terrorism and those that sponsor it. Two incidents are used for purposes of illustration: the U.S. interception of the Egyptian airliner carrying the hijackers of the *Achille Lauro* to safe haven, and the U.S. bombing raid against Libya.

Interception of the Egyptian Airliner

On October 7, 1985, Palestinian terrorists hijacked the Italian cruise liner *Achille Lauro* and, during the course of hijacking, brutally murdered Leon Klinghoffer, a 69-year-old American Jew in a wheelchair. When the ship docked in Port Said, the hostages were released, but the terrorists were not turned over to the appropriate Egyptian authorities for prosecution. Instead the Egyptian government com-

mandeered a civilian aircraft to fly the terrorists to a safe haven.
However, on October 10, four U.S. military aircraft intercepted the
Egyptian airliner over the Mediterranean Sea and compelled it to
change course and land in Italy, where four of the alleged hijackers
were taken into custody by local authorities.[28]

The U.S. government offered no legal justification for its interception of the Egyptian plane, which Schachter has contended was
illegal.[29] But his argument has certain flaws.[30] Schachter argues that
the interception violated rules of civil aviation agreements prohibiting
interception of civilian aircraft over the high seas.[31] But state
aircraft—defined as aircraft used in military, police, and customs
services—are excluded from the scope of the Convention on International Civil Aviation (the Chicago Convention), the primary agreement in the field.[32] Although the airliner carrying the hijackers of
the *Achille Lauro* was normally engaged in civil aviation, in this
instance it was engaged in a special police mission; the plane therefore
should be classified as a state aircraft and not within the scope of
the Chicago Convention.

It might also be claimed that the U.S. interception violated the
customary international law principle of freedom of overflight of
the high seas, which is also recognized in article 2 of the Geneva
Convention on the High Seas.[33] This principle, however, is not
absolute and would seem inapplicable when a state aircraft is on a
special mission designed to facilitate the escape of terrorists. Under
article 105 of the UN Convention on the Law of the Sea,[34] which
repeats article 19 of the Geneva Convention on the High Seas and
is declaratory of customary law, any state may seize a "pirate ship
or aircraft" (or a ship seized by pirates and under their control)
and arrest the wrongdoers on board. Professor Schachter suggests
that "the fact that a state's vessel or plane is carrying 'pirates' (or
terrorists) and intends to release them does not transform the vessel
or plane into a 'pirate' ship or aircraft."[35] In principle, however, it
is not clear why such a plane or ship should not be so regarded,
at least when it is on a special mission whose sole purpose is to
allow the terrorists to escape from the scene of their crimes. This
situation would seem distinguishable from the case in which alleged
terrorists are on a civilian flight that is intercepted over the high
seas, in which case the Chicago Convention would clearly be ap-

plicable—the danger to innocent passengers and crew would override the need to apprehend and prosecute the terrorists for their crimes.

Professor Schachter also suggests that the U.S. action violated article 2(4) of the UN Charter, which provides that "[a]ll members shall refrain in their international relations from the threat or use of force against the territorial integrity or political independence of any state, or in any other manner inconsistent with the Purposes of the United Nations." To be sure, as Schachter has pointed out, "[i]t is generally assumed that the prohibition [of article 2(4)] was intended to preclude all use of force except that allowed as self-defense or authorized by the Security Council under Chapter VII of the Charter. Yet the article was not drafted that way. The last twenty-three words contain qualifications."[36] He also notes that governments and scholars, as well as the International Court of Justice in the *Corfu Channel Case*,[37] have rejected the argument that the qualifying language of article 2(4) justifies the use of force solely to vindicate or secure a legal right, on the ground that it is not directed against the territorial integrity or political independence of a state and it is consistent with UN purposes. Hence it would follow that the United States could not use armed force against Egypt on the sole ground that Egypt had failed to fulfill its obligations under the Hostages Convention. Nor, a fortiori, could the United States use force against Egypt by way of reprisal for its violation of that convention.

The *Achille Lauro* situation, however, may present a special case. Arguably, Egypt had not only failed to fulfill its obligations under the Hostages Convention, but had also become an accomplice of the terrorists by providing them with a plane to take them to safe haven. Under these circumstances, the United States may have been entitled to use force limited to the extent reasonable under the circumstances. It is important to note that the threat of force was not directed against Egyptian territory or against Egypt's political structure. Nor was this threat of force, designed to prevent the escape of terrorists, inconsistent with the purposes of the United Nations. Moreover, nations arguably can threaten more force than they can use.[38] Had the U.S. planes fired on the Egyptian airliner, a more difficult case would have been presented.

If we assume that article 2(4) of the UN Charter should be interpreted as prohibiting any threat or use of force except in self-defense or in accordance with an authorization from the Security Council, a good case can be made that the U.S. action was justifiable under article 51 of the Charter, which declares that "[n]othing in the present Charter shall impair the inherent right of individual or collective self-defense if an armed attack occurs." Although the point is debatable, the taking of American hostages and the murder of Leon Klinghoffer on the *Achille Lauro* arguably constituted an armed attack on the United States. Moreover, the right to use force in response continued as long as the incident was still in progress and the hijackers were attempting to escape. Recourse to peaceful means had been exhausted when Egypt declined to extradite or prosecute the terrorists and instead participated in their attempt to escape. Time did not permit recourse to the Security Council, which would have been futile in any event. The use of force was thus necessary to prevent the escape of the terrorists. In addition, it was the minimum amount necessary to effect the capture and therefore proportionate to the goal. Finally, it did not constitute a reprisal because there was no punitive intent with regard to Egypt.[39]

The U.S. Bombing Raid Against Libya

The U.S. bombing raid against Libya on April 15, 1986, is to date the only attack made directly against a state for its sponsoring of terrorism. Somewhat surprisingly, the U.S. action has not stimulated much commentary about the legal aspects,[40] nor has the U.S. government provided much by way of legal justification for the attack.[41] It is not the purpose of this section of the chapter to fill the gap. Rather, the purpose here is to address a few of the salient issues the raid raises and to set forth some tentative conclusions.

Most observers would contend that a bombing raid against the territory of a state constitutes a prima facie violation of article 2(4) of the UN Charter. But, the legality of the raid would appear to turn on whether it can be defended as an act of self-defense under article 51 of the Charter, which provides:

> Nothing in the present Charter shall impair the inherent right of individual or collective self-defense if an armed attack occurs against a Member of the United Nations, until the Security Council has taken the measures necessary to maintain international peace and security.

Measures taken by members in the exercise of this right of self-defense shall be immediately reported to the Security Council and shall not in any way affect the authority and responsibility of the Security Council under the present Charter to take at any time such action as it deems necessary in order to maintain or restore international peace and security.

There has long been a debate in the scholarly literature and elsewhere over the precise meaning and scope of article 51. One issue has been whether article 51 is merely a "savings clause," preserving the right of self-defense as it existed prior to the Charter, or whether the words "armed attack" were intended to place further limits on the right to use force in self-defense. The 1986 decision of the International Court of Justice in *Nicaragua v. United States*[42] addressed this issue and reached some startling conclusions.

In *Nicaragua v. United States,* the ICJ not only concluded that the words "armed attack" place additional constraints on the use of force in self-defense; the court defined these words so narrowly as to imply that their coverage would be limited to a state sending armed bands across international boundaries. Specifically, the court stated that a number of actions—including the supply of weapons to insurgents in another state—might constitute a violation of article 2(4), but do not amount to an "armed attack" within the meaning of article 51. Not having suffered an "armed attack," the state which is facing an attack from insurgents cannot invoke article 51 as a justification for striking back militarily against the state supplying them. The court indicated, cryptically, that the victim state might nonetheless be entitled to employ "proportional countermeasures" that might themselves include the use of force, although the court found it unnecessary to decide this issue in the present case. In any event, these "proportionate countermeasures" could be employed only by the victim state itself and not by any third state (the United States) as an act of collective self-defense.

The highly debatable nature of this dictum has not gone unnoticed. In the words of Thomas Franck:

Thus, the Court was able to conclude that "under international law in force today—whether customary international law or that of the United Nations system—States do not have a right of 'collective'

armed response to acts which do not constitute an 'armed attack.'"
In the majority's view, "only when the wrongful act provoking the
response was an armed attack," i.e., something reaching the threshold
of the dispatch of armed bands "on a significant scale," may the
United States go to the aid of an El Salvador by giving aid to an
insurgency in a Nicaragua. This seemingly rigid barrier is slightly
dented by a vague assertion that there may, in undefined circumstances,
be "some right analogous to the right of collective self-defence" against
a level of intervention falling short of an actual "armed attack."

The consequence of this substantive rule appears to be that fire
may be fought with water, but not with fire. It is a proposition that
leaves victimized states little option but to confine countermeasures
to their own territory, where, it appears, they may secure the aid of
friendly states in dealing with insurgents. They are not, however,
allowed to strike back at the base camps, the source of their troubles,
in the states sponsoring proxy civil war, at least not until the intervention
reaches the "armed attack" threshold defined by the Court. Source
states get a free ride, legally invulnerable to individual or collective
response against their own territory, even if the insurgency is planned,
trained, armed and directed from there.[43]

Moreover, John Lawrence Hargrove has pointed out that the court's
dictum is inconsistent with the UN Charter, with the experience of
states, and with the development of customary international law by
such UN organs as the Security Council and the General Assembly.
He suggests that instead

> The Court should simply have stuck to the Charter: if Nicaragua
> used unlawful force, it should be held accountable, and the victim
> and any other state acting in concert with it held entitled to defend
> against that conduct with proportionate force to the extent necessary
> to put an end to it. If the United States used more force than was
> reasonably necessary for that purpose, or was not really acting in
> concert with a victim state, it acted unlawfully and should be held
> accountable. If the Court for whatever reason could not or did not
> obtain adequate evidence to make a responsible determination of this
> grave issue between sovereign states, it should have declined to
> determine it.[44]

In fairness it should be pointed out that other eminent authorities
have applauded the court's interpretation of article 51,[45] although

if it is correct, the burden of proof on the United States to justify its attack against Libya would seem substantial.

Even under the ICJ's onerous standard, there is a case to be made in support of the legality of the U.S. strike. According to Abraham Sofaer, the State Department's legal adviser, there was "strong evidence of some 30 possible impending Libyan attacks on U.S. facilities and personnel throughout the world. The April 14 strikes were to deter these and other planned attacks."[46] If that intelligence information was correct, the imminence of these attacks, which would have been taken pursuant to Libyan direction and control, might have justified the U.S. response—although even this conclusion is questionable in light of the court's restrictive interpretation. Under the traditional approach to article 51, however, the U.S. action would seem authorized by customary international law, which allows an armed response if the "necessity of that self-defence is instant, overwhelming, and leaving no choice of means, and no moment for deliberation."[47] As Dean Acheson once remarked, "The law is not a suicide pact," yet any formulation of article 51 that would preclude a state from resorting to force in the kind of situation described by Sofaer would seem to amount to such a pact.

One of the many difficulties in analyzing the U.S. attack against Libya is that there is disagreement over the facts in the case. Some have questioned Sofaer's allegation that widespread attacks by Libya against U.S. property and nationals were imminent. This dispute over the facts demonstrates the need (discussed in previous chapters) for improved multilateral gathering, dissemination, and analysis of intelligence data. A multilateral determination of Libya's sponsorship of terrorism along the lines alleged by Sofaer and the State Department would have lent a substantial measure of authoritative support to the substantive conclusions reached unilaterally by the United States.

Assuming *arguendo* that the United States could legally resort to the use of armed force against Libya consistent with the constraints of article 51, there are two other issues arising out of the U.S. attack. The first concerns the way the attack was carried out. According to U.S. official statements, only military facilities and terrorist training camps were targeted. Nonetheless, the bombing was less accurate than anticipated, which resulted in the destruction of civilian residences and loss of civilian lives. Commenting on this fact in a speech before the National War College, Keith Highet contended:

> Even assuming—for the sake of this discussion—that the evidence of linkage between the terrorist bombings and the sponsoring State was sufficiently established by clear and objective evidence (and there is considerable doubt about the Libyan example), there was still an impossibly heavy burden placed on the United States by the fact that the operation involved deliberately attacking targets in built-up civilian areas. The targets may have been military, but their location within civilian areas, and the time and nature of the attack, made it almost impossible to satisfy the test of proportionality or reasonableness of response that must be met whenever self-defensive action (or retaliatory or preemptive action) is undertaken using deadly force. As it was, a large number of civilian casualties occurred in those attacks, and any short-term objective of discouraging State-sponsored terrorism must be weighed against our interest in compliance with the rule of law. We will doubtless come to regret it.[48]

Reasonable persons may differ over Highet's conclusion that the nature of the attack meant it failed to satisfy the test of proportionality. More troubling is the allegation by Seymour Hersh, in the *New York Times Magazine,* that the intent of the Reagan administration in the bombing of Libya was to kill Muammar Qadhafi.[49] That is, the intent allegedly was to hit his tent, which housed his wife and various children as well as Qadhafi. Assassination of a state's leaders undertaken at the direction of another state clearly violates a number of international law norms and doctrines.[50] It is, moreover, prohibited by presidential executive order.[51] Assassination by a bombing attack is also less discriminate than assassination by a "hit squad," and the question that arises is whether an intent to kill Qadhafi with the likelihood of killing members of his family as well is consistent with the law of armed conflict.

The second issue in the case of the U.S. bombing of Libya is whether the United States had fulfilled its obligation under the UN Charter to exhaust all means for the peaceful resolution of disputes. Especially disquieting in this respect is that the administration on March 23, 1986, sent a large fleet into the Gulf of Sidra (claimed by Libya as its territorial waters on the basis of historical title) to conduct major naval exercises.[52] In response, Libya launched abortive attacks against U.S. planes. Soon after, U.S. ships and planes attacked three Libyan patrol boats, sinking two and damaging the other. Only thereafter, on March 25, 1986, did U.S. Ambassador Walters send a letter to the president of the Security Council.[53]

In his letter, Ambassador Walters argued that U.S. forces were acting in self-defense under article 51 and that when they were attacked, U.S. ships and planes were on or above international waters and were exercising their freedom of navigation under international law. He also pointed out that the United States had filed notification of intent to conduct those exercises with the ICAO and contended that Libya had no valid claim to control navigation through these international waters. In conclusion, he suggested that in view of the grave challenge to freedom of navigation in international waters posed by Libya's actions, the Security Council should reaffirm the internationally accepted freedoms of navigation and overflight.

It is at best disingenuous for Ambassador Walters to describe Libya's claim to the Gulf of Sidra as a "grave challenge to freedom of navigation in international waters" or the administration's sending of an armada into the Gulf of Sidra as necessary to uphold freedom of navigation and overflight of the high seas. The Gulf of Sidra can hardly be described as an important route of international navigation. Moreover, it was unnecessary for the United States to send an entire battle group into the area to maintain its claim that the Gulf of Sidra encompasses international waters. Libya's claim enjoys no significant support—a simple protest to it would have been sufficient to preserve the U.S. legal position.[54] Most important, if this dispute were really over the status of the waters in the Gulf of Sidra, this would seem an issue especially suitable for reference to the International Court of Justice or to international arbitration.[55] Nor is it a foregone conclusion that Libya would have refused to submit the dispute to the ICJ, since it has agreed to the court's jurisdiction over law of the sea issues in the past.[56]

It is also arguable that the United States failed to exhaust other possible means of peaceful resolution of its specific dispute with Libya over its support of terrorism, especially reference to the Security Council, before resorting to the use of armed force. This is not to say that the United States was required to turn to the Security Council or any other political organ or judicial tribunal if—as alleged by Sofaer—armed attacks against U.S. personnel and property were imminent. But prior to receiving evidence of imminent terrorist attacks sponsored by Libya, the United States did not bring the issue of Libyan sponsorship of terrorism before the United Nations. Nor is it any defense to argue that efforts to settle these disputes peacefully with Libya would have been futile.[57] The language of the UN Charter is categorical; peaceful means for the resolution of disputes, including reference of the dispute to the Security Council if other methods fail, "shall" be employed.[58] The rationale behind this mandate is that it prevents states from unilaterally determining that resort to peaceful mechanisms of dispute settlement would be futile. Any other approach would seriously undermine the UN's ability to perform its primary function: the maintenance of international peace and security.

To be sure, in the four months prior to the attack, the United States initiated a number of diplomatic and economic measures with respect to Libya because of its support of terrorism,[59] none of which had any discernible effect. But it is unfortunate that the United States did not turn as well to the United Nations. Too often in that organization the United States has appeared, in effect, as a defendant. As suggested previously, the United States should bring charges before the UN General Assembly and the Security Council—backed by as much intelligence data as can be offered consistent with the need to protect intelligence sources—against state sponsors of terrorism. The "struggle for law" currently taking place in those organs demands no less.

Conclusion

Under certain circumstances, the use of armed force can be a legally permissible response to state-sponsored terrorism. This is the case whether the use of force is undertaken as part of a rescue mission or in response to an imminent or actual terrorist armed attack sponsored by a state. At the same time, the use of armed force should be reserved for truly exceptional circumstances requiring an act of self-defense. Moreover, in the absence of an imminent armed attack, all possible methods of peaceful resolution of disputes, including recourse to the UN Security Council, should be exhausted.

Support for the use of armed force will inexorably intensify if peaceful responses to state-sponsored terrorism prove unsuccessful. Hence, every effort should be made to ensure their effectiveness.

Notes

1. The following discussion is drawn largely from Murphy, *State Self-Help and Problems of Public International Law*, LEGAL ASPECTS OF INTERNATIONAL TERRORISM 553, 554–62 (A. Evans & J. Murphy eds. 1978).

2. *See* W. STEVENSON, 90 MINUTES AT ENTEBBE 27 (1976).

3. *Id.* at 172.

4. *Id.* at 174.

5. *See Statement by Ambassador Scranton*, 74 DEP'T STATE BULL. 181 (Aug. 2, 1976).

6. 13 U.N. MONTHLY CHRONICLE 15 (Aug.-Sept. 1976).

7. *Statement by Ambassador Bennett*, 74 DEP'T STATE BULL. 185 (Aug. 2, 1976).

8. *Id.*

9. N.Y. Times, July 16, 1976, at A20, col. 3.

10. *See generally* Frank & Rodley, *After Bangledesh: The Law of Humanitarian Intervention by Military Force*, 67 AM. J. INT'L L. 275 (1973).

11. *See* 12 M. WHITEMAN, DIGEST OF INTERNATIONAL LAW 204–15 (1971).

12. Frank & Rodley, *supra* note 10, at 304.

13. *See* 12 WHITEMAN, *supra* note 11, at 77–79.

14. *Id.* at 77–84.

15. *Id.*

16. M. MCDOUGAL & F. FELICIANO, LAW AND MINIMUM WORLD PUBLIC ORDER 248 (1961).

17. D. BOWETT, SELF-DEFENCE IN INTERNATIONAL LAW 201–02 (1958).

18. W. PROSSER & P. KEETON, THE LAW OF TORTS 130 (5th ed. 1984).

19. Waldock, *The Regulation of the Use of Force by Individual States in International Law*, 136 RECUEIL DES COURS 411, 467 (1972 vol. 2).

20. A. ROSS, THE UNITED NATIONS: PEACE AND PROGRESS 209 (1966).

21. *See generally* Note, *The Congo Crisis 1964: A Case Study in Humanitarian Intervention*, 12 VA. J. INT'L. L. 261 (1972).

22. For a detailed discussion of the crisis, *see* Schachter, *Self-Help in International Law: U.S. Action in the Iranian Hostages Crisis*, 37 J. INT'L AFF. 231 (1984).

23. *Id.*

24. Case Concerning United States Diplomatic and Consular Staff in Teheran (U.S. V. Iran), 1979 I.C.J. Rep. 7 (Order of Provisional Measures, Dec. 15, 1979).

25. *See* Schachter, *supra* note 22, at 243–44.

26. *Id.* at 244–45.

27. *Id.* at 242–43.

28. Most of the discussion in this section is drawn from Murphy, *The Future of Multilateralism and Efforts to Combat International Terrorism*, 25 COLUM. J. TRANSNAT'L L. 35, 80–83 (1986).

29. *See* Schachter, *In Defense of International Rules on the Use of Force*, 53 U. CHI. L. REV. 113, 140 (1986).

30. *See* Murphy, *supra* note 28, at 81, fn. 218.

31. *See, e.g.,* Convention on International Civil Aviation, Dec. 7, 1944, 61 Stat. 1180, T.I.A.S. No. 1591, 15 U.N.T.S. 295.

32. *See id.* art. 3.

33. Geneva Convention on the High Seas, April 29, 1958, 13 U.S.T. 2312, 2314, T.I.A.S. No. 5200, at 3, 450 U.N.T.S. 82, 83.

34. U.N. Doc. A/Conf. 62/122 (1982), *reprinted in* 21 I.L.M. 1261, 1289 (1982).

35. Schachter, *supra* note 29, at 140.

36. Schachter, *The Right of States to Use Armed Force*, 82 MICH. L. REV. 1620, 1625 (1984).

37. The Corfu Channel Case (U.K. v. Alb.), 1949 I.C.J. Rep. 4 (Judgment of April 9).

38. *See Report of the Committee on the Use of Force in Relations Among States,* PROCEEDINGS OF THE AMERICAN BRANCH OF THE INTERNATIONAL LAW ASSOCIATION 188, 195 (1985–86).

39. Professor Schachter has suggested that a temporal element inheres in the right to self-defense; that is, any response must be made close in time to an attack or imminent threat. Schachter, *supra* note 29, at 132. The attack on the U.S. hostages had ended, but was still close in time to the interception of the Egyptian airplane.

40. Some examples of this relatively limited commentary include several articles in 19 CASE W. RES. J. INT'L L. 121–293 (1987); Boyle, *Preserving the Rule of Law in the War Against International Terrorism*, 8 WHITTIER L. REV. 735 (1986); Thornberry, *International Law and Its Discontents: The U.S. Raid on Libya*, 8 LIVERPOOL L. REV. 53 (1986).

41. The primary legal defense of the raid by the U.S. government is to be found in Sofaer, *Terrorism and the Law*, 64 FOREIGN AFF. 901, 921 (1986).

42. Military and Paramilitary Activities in and Against Nicaragua (Nicar. v. U.S.), Merits, 1986 I.C.J. Rep. 14 (Judgment of June 27).

43. Franck, *Some Observations on the ICJ's Procedural and Substantive Innovations*, 81 AM. J. INT'L L. 116, 120 (1987).

44. Hargrove, *The Nicaragua Judgment and the Future of the Law of Force and Self-Defense*, 81 AM. J. INT'L L. 135, 143 (1987).

45. *See e.g.*, Briggs, *The International Court of Justice Lives Up to Its Name*, 81 AM. J. INT'L L. 78 (1987); Falk, *The World Court's Achievement, id.* at 106.

46. Sofaer, *supra* note 41, at 921.

47. This formulation appeared in a diplomatic note by U.S. Secretary of State Daniel Webster to the British in 1842. Webster's note was a response to Britain's claim that it had a legal right to attack a vessel (the *Caroline*) on the American side of the Niagara River in 1837 because the ship carried armed men intending to use force to support an insurrection in Canada. *See* 2 MOORE, DIGEST OF INTERNATIONAL LAW 412 (1906).

48. Address by Keith Highet to the National War College, Aug. 19, 1987. A copy of his speech is in my files.

49. Hersh, *Target Qaddafi*, N.Y. Times Magazine, Feb. 22, 1987, at 16, col. 1.

50. For discussion, *see* MURPHY, THE UNITED NATIONS AND THE CONTROL OF INTERNATIONAL VIOLENCE 179–80 (1982).

51. Exec. Order No. 12,333, 3 C.F.R. 200 (1981).

52. Much of the following discussion is drawn from Murphy, *The Future of Multilateralism and Efforts to Combat International Terrorism*, 25 COLUM. J. TRANSNAT'L L. 35, 87–88 (1986).

53. 86 DEP'T STATE BULL. 80 (1986).

54. For a discussion of the Libyan claim to the Gulf of Sidra, *see* Blum, *The Gulf of Sidra Incident*, 80 AM. J. INT'L L. 668 (1986).

55. Article 36, para. 3, of the UN Charter provides that in making recommendations, the Security Council "should also take into consideration that legal disputes should as a general rule be referred by the parties to the International Court of Justice in accordance with the provisions of the Statute of the Court."

56. *See* Case Concerning the Continental Shelf (Tunisia v. Libyan Arab Jamahiriya), 1982 I.C.J. Rep. 18.

57. For an example of such an argument, *see* Intoccia, *American Bombing of Libya: An International Legal Analysis*, 19 CASE W. RES. 177, 207–08 (1987).

58. U.N. CHARTER, art. 37, para. 1.

59. For a discussion of these measures, *see* Intoccia, *supra* note 57, at 208–09.

7

Some Concluding Notes

This final chapter turns first to general conclusions and recommendations that transcend the particular topics previously addressed. It then presents an overview of the individual chapters in an effort to glean from them conclusions and recommendations especially worthy of attention.

General Conclusions

By definition, terrorism involves a political dimension. This political dimension has been a major obstacle to efforts (inside and outside the United Nations) to combat terrorism. Insofar as these efforts have been successful, they have downplayed the political elements of the problem by focusing on those aspects of terrorist acts that warrant their being treated as crimes. The approach has been to emphasize the impermissibility and hence criminal nature of aircraft hijacking and sabotage, attacks on diplomats, hostage taking, hijacking of and other attacks on shipping, and theft of nuclear material.

The political dimension of terrorism is compounded when a state chooses to support or sponsor terrorist acts, circumstances that make it impossible to treat the problem simply as a matter of criminal law. Difficult issues of public international law necessarily arise—especially in the more serious case of state sponsorship—concerning the maintenance of international peace and security.

The highly charged political dimension of state-sponsored terrorism undermines efforts to combat it in many ways. For example, intelligence information—difficult to gather, disseminate, and analyze with respect to even purely private acts of international terrorism—

may become increasingly elusive when state sponsorship is present. The state sponsor may use its own intelligence agencies to destroy evidence of its involvement or to engage in "disinformation" campaigns to compromise reliability of the data. Further, states heavily involved economically or politically with the sponsor state may be reluctant to share intelligence in their possession, even if they would have no such hesitation with respect to intelligence concerning purely private acts.

Definitional difficulties also are exacerbated when a state is involved. Chapter 1 explores the problem of defining terrorism in some detail. This problem is complicated, and new definitional problems introduced, when state sponsorship intrudes. The terms "state support" and "state sponsorship" are almost as difficult to define as "terrorism," and the three concepts are inextricably intertwined in a complex matrix. The relationship between these terms is explored extensively in Chapter 2, and we return to it in the next section.

The possible responses to state-supported or state-sponsored terrorism explored in Chapters 3 through 6 depend for their effectiveness on cooperation among like-minded states, but such cooperation may be lacking because of special political relations between the state sponsor and the states whose cooperation is essential to the success of the contemplated responses. The political problems of dealing with state-sponsored terrorism can best be countered through the political process. Through diplomatic demarches, every effort should be made to convince states reluctant to take steps to counter state sponsorship that regardless of their relationship with a state sponsor, they should be willing to take a strong stand against its sponsorship of clearly impermissible acts of terrorism. We return to this theme in the next section also.

As to possible responses to terrorism, the major emphasis should be on finding more creative ways to respond other than through the use of armed force. Although in a particular instance it may be legally defensible, resort to the use of armed force usually represents a failure of the international legal process. The preeminent policy of modern international law, as reflected in the United Nations Charter and other international law instruments, is the settlement of disputes between states by peaceful means. Article 51 of the UN

Charter is, in effect, a savings clause that permits resort to force, but only if necessity permits no other recourse.

Specific Conclusions

Definitional Problems

As Chapter 1 demonstrates, no agreed-upon definition of "terrorism" has been reached, at either the international or national level. But it is unnecessary for purposes of this book to choose from among the various definitions proposed. From a functional perspective, terrorism should be defined as (a) those acts already covered by the antiterrorist conventions or (b) those identified by a substantial majority of the world community as impermissible under any circumstances, a category that particularly includes the deliberate targeting of unarmed civilians and the theft of nuclear material usable for military purposes.

This narrow definition of terrorism seems most functional for purposes of seeking international cooperation against terrorism. Evidence that a state has supported or sponsored acts that fair-minded persons would agree are legally and morally impermissible greatly strengthens the case for taking measures against this state— especially measures of a more coercive nature, such as economic sanctions.

In the same vein, "state sponsorship" should be defined narrowly and limited to situations in which the state contributes active planning, direction, and control to terrorist operations. "State support" should be defined much more broadly, along the lines discussed in Chapter 2, and would include actions taken even by states friendly to the United States, including the release of terrorist suspects and the grant of safe haven.

Intelligence and State Support
of International Terrorism

As noted in the first section of this chapter, political difficulties in obtaining intelligence about terrorism are compounded when a state supports terrorist acts. In addition, state involvement raises the issue of whether Interpol can reconcile an intelligence function with article 3 of its constitution, which precludes that organization from undertaking any activities of "a political, military, religious or racial character."

There is general agreement among law enforcement and intelligence officers that informal links between these two groups is preferable to a highly structured international organization. In recent years, these informal ties have been strengthened, and cooperation between U.S. and foreign intelligence officers has increased. Nonetheless, there are indications that even these informal working groups could benefit from the development of guidelines to provide a framework for their activities. Interpol has recently developed some guidelines[1] that might serve as a model for the less structured groups.

Moreover, a 1988 conference cosponsored by the Rand Corporation and the Department of State[2] (hereafter "Rand Conference") identified additional problems and discussed some steps for their resolution. There was general agreement, for example, on the need to eliminate or at least minimize jurisdictional disputes among intelligence, law enforcement, and military agencies at the national level. The situation in the United States was perceived as especially unsatisfactory in this regard. Several participants suggested that international intelligence working groups might address this problem, since divisiveness at the national level hampers the effectiveness of international cooperation.

As discussed at some length in Chapter 3, ambiguities in national law and policy raise the issue of whether there is currently an appropriate balance struck between providing law enforcement and security officials with sufficient authority and guidelines to discharge their responsibilities for combatting terrorist activities and yet to ensure the protection of such fundamental values as freedom of information and privacy. Participants at the Rand Conference were of the view that this issue might usefully be considered in the international working groups (in order to introduce a comparative law perspective) and that these groups might also attempt to draft model legislation as a guide for the revision or adoption of national legislation. Harmonization of national law and practice in the intelligence area was perceived as greatly needed.

There was also a common perception at the Rand Conference of a need for more joint training of intelligence officers from different countries and even of a need for cross-border intelligence operations.

This, in the view of several participants, would maximize the sharing of intelligence and operational effectiveness. (One participant noted that intelligence regarding state sponsorship of terrorism is seldom shared because a sympathetic state may leak the information to the sponsor.)

Finally, it was pointed out that there is a need for greater coordination between immigration and consular authorities and intelligence officials, especially with respect to the sharing of intelligence. The usefulness of immigration and visa controls in preventing the entry of terrorists into a country and leading to their arrest and prosecution is just beginning to be appreciated.

Quiet Diplomacy, Public Protest,
and International and Transnational Claims

In any formulation of possible responses to state-supported or sponsored terrorism, it is important to note that diplomacy is an extremely important—arguably the most important—method for dealing with the problem. The examples of diplomatic successes discussed in Chapter 4 reveal the benefits to be derived from using as intermediaries states enjoying close relations with states that sponsor terrorism to induce them to cease such sponsorship. Greater use should be made of such intermediaries.[3] Moreover, an effort should be made to regularize the use of intermediaries, rather than to turn to them on an ad hoc, reactive basis. Demarches by state intermediaries are likely to be most effective if made in situations in which a state is contemplating sponsoring terrorism but has not yet made a decision to do so.

If quiet diplomacy fails, public protest may be useful to bring the glare of publicity—as an exercise in the "mobilization of shame" often used effectively with respect to egregious violations of human rights—to bear on a state sponsor of terrorism. Every effort should be made to make this protest as multilateral as possible.

The bringing of international and transnational claims may be a more realistic response to state-sponsored terrorism than is commonly supposed. With respect to international claims, it is important to note that they may be brought in political arenas, such as the UN Security Council or General Assembly, as well as before an international arbitral tribunal or an international court. Protests set forth in diplomatic correspondence or raised in international organizations should fully state the facts and law proving a violation of international law and challenge the accused state to refute them. A strong case that peremptory norms of international law have been violated lends a substantial measure of weight to a diplomatic protest and may lay the foundation for other responses should the state responsible fail to desist from its sponsorship. The prospect for success in bringing claims before an international arbitral or judicial tribunal are problematic but should not be ruled out on an a priori basis. As discussed in Chapter 4, there are examples of past successes in bringing such claims, and there may be similar opportunities in the future.

The most promising prospect for international adjudicatory remedies may lie in actions against states that, by their failure to fulfill their international obligations, merely support rather than sponsor terrorism. The possibility of such states agreeing to the jurisdiction of the tribunal might be greater than it would be in cases against states sponsoring terrorism. In this connection, consideration might be given to the bringing of a claim before a regional tribunal, such as the European Court of Human Rights or the European Court of Justice. Such actions would have to be brought by states other than the United States, since it is not a party to either the European Convention on Human Rights or the Rome Treaty.

As noted in Chapter 4, the possibility of obtaining civil remedies in national courts against terrorists and the states sponsoring them is a subject that is just beginning to receive systematic attention. This should continue and intensify. The final decision in *Klinghoffer v. Palestine Liberation Organization*[4] should clarify the extent to which civil remedies may be available in U.S. courts against terrorists and terrorist organizations. The Foreign Sovereign Immunities Act (FSIA) currently bars any civil suits against state sponsors of international terrorism.[5] Some have suggested that the act be amended to permit such suits.

In my opinion, FSIA should not be amended to remove a state's immunity in the event it sponsors international terrorism. Although this proposal has its attractions, especially in light of the problematic nature of international judicial remedies, the risks that implementation of such a proposal would raise substantially outweigh the benefits that might be gained. Specifically, the potential adverse impact that suits brought in domestic courts against state sponsors of terrorism might have on the foreign relations of the United States would be considerable. Such proceedings, moreover, could result in retaliatory actions against the United States in the courts of other countries that might be inclined to define terrorism and state sponsorship of it quite differently from any definition appearing in U.S. legislation or adopted by U.S. courts.

It should be noted that the issues surrounding suits in U.S. courts against state sponsors of international terrorism are quite different from the issues raised in *Klinghoffer v. Palestine Liberation Organization.* Strong arguments can be made that victims of terrorism such as the Klinghoffers should have available to them civil remedies in U.S. courts against private individuals or organizations that commit or sponsor terrorist acts. A working group established by the American Bar Association's Standing Committee on Law and National Security has drafted an International Terrorism Civil Liability Act that would provide for such remedies.[6] Although even here there might be a danger of retaliatory suits in foreign courts against U.S. citizens and organizations, my tentative conclusion is that the risk is worth taking.

Economic Sanctions

As the discussion in Chapter 5 indicates, recent studies have cast doubt on the conventional wisdom that economic sanctions are ineffective as a remedy against states that violate international law. With specific reference to state sponsors of terrorism, the multilateral sanctions employed against Syria and the Bonn Declaration sanctions threatened against South Africa seem to have had considerable effect.

Chapter 5 recommends that the United States and like-minded states explore the possibility of concluding a convention that would require states that are parties to impose draconian sanctions against a state determined by an independent tribunal to be sponsoring terrorism. The Draft Convention for the Suppression of State-Sponsored Terrorism proposed by Keith Highet to the American Society of International Law's Committee on Responses to State-Sponsored Terrorism might serve as a guide to this effort. The reasons supporting this recommendation are set forth in Chapter 5 and will not be repeated here. It is worth noting, however, that

at an ICAO-sponsored conference in 1973, the United States and
like-minded states endorsed the idea of a sanctions convention against
states that supported aircraft hijacking.[7] This draft convention provided for a fact-finding commission to determine whether a state
had failed either to extradite a hijacker found within its territory
or to submit the case to its competent authorities for the purpose
of prosecution. In the event of such a determination, states parties
to the convention would have been required to take joint action,
including the suspension of all international aviation to and from
the defaulting state.

Hence there is precedent for the United States and states with
similar views to agree to a convention against states that support
terrorism. Moreover, the convention proposed by Highet would be
limited in its application to the most egregious instances of state-
supported international terrorism. Here, as discussed in Chapter 5,
the moral case for the imposition of severe economic sanctions is
especially compelling.

The Use of Armed Force

As stated in Chapter 6, I believe that article 51 of the United
Nations Charter does permit the use of force as an act of self-
defense against a state that sponsors terrorist attacks—at least if
these attacks are substantial and have actually taken place or are
imminent. The dictum of the International Court of Justice in
Nicaragua v. United States apparently defining the term "armed attack"
so narrowly as to exclude most uses of armed force (other than the
sending of armies across international borders) does not reflect the
law of the UN Charter or sound legal policy.

At the same time, the use of armed force against state sponsors
of terrorism is normally undesirable, and thus much greater emphasis
should be placed on the peaceful responses to state-sponsored terrorism discussed in this book. The hope is that the more creative
use of these alternative methods of response will obviate the use of
armed force. If this hope goes unrealized, the likelihood of further
use of armed force against state sponsors of terrorism will be great—
and the human suffering in turn considerable.

Notes

1. The Interpol guidelines were distributed at the Conference on Practical Methods to Fight Terrorism, held April 28–29, 1988, in Washington, D.C., and cosponsored by the Rand Corporation and the Department of State.

2. *See supra* note 1.

3. Algeria recently played a mediator's role in obtaining the release of passengers on a hijacked Kuwait airplane in exchange for release of hijackers with the agreement of the Kuwait government. See N.Y. Times, April 21, 1988, at A1, col. 1.

4. Klinghoffer v. Palestine Liberation Organization, 27801/85 (N.Y. Sup. Ct.).

5. In Tel-Oren v. Libya, 726 F.2d 774, 755–776, 805 (D.C. Cir. 1984), both Judge Robert Bork and Judge Harry Edwards, in footnotes, summarily dismissed a suit against Libya based on sponsorship of terrorism on the ground it was barred by the Foreign Sovereign Immunities Act. Also, in Argentine Republic v. Amerada Hess, 57 U.S. Law Week 4121 (Jan. 23, 1989), the Supreme Court unanimously reversed a decision of the Second Circuit that a state may not claim sovereign immunity under FSIA for a violation of the law of nations.

6. By early 1989 the draft statute had not yet been considered by the Standing Committee.

7. For a thorough discussion of this proposal for a convention on sanctions, *see* Chamberlain, *Collective Suspension of Air Services with States Which Harbour Hijackers,* 32 INT'L & COMP. L.Q. 616, 618 (1983).

Index